CULTURES OF THE WORLD®

CUBA

Sean Sheehan & Leslie Jermyn

Marshall Cavendish
Benchmark

New York

PICTURE CREDITS

Cover photo: © Getty Images: Angelo Cavalli
AFP: 28, 34 • Bes Stock: 56 • Camera Press: 25, 102 • Douglas Donne Bryant Stock
Photography: 24, 39, 40, 46, 76, 79, 98, 99, 109 • Eye Ubiquitous: 6 • HBL Network: 53,
122 • Houserstock Inc.: 1, 5, 51, 106 • Hutchison Library: 65, 100, 111, 119, 126 • The
Image Bank: 27, 60 • John R. Jones: 50, 55 • Björn Klingwall: 7, 15, 20, 31, 43, 45, 68,
77, 83 • Life File Photo Library: 35, 59, 64, 67, 72, 75, 84, 89, 91, 92, 95, 128 • Lonely
Planet Images: 52, 54, 66, 88, 94, 114, 125 • Keith Mundy: 90, 105 • Keith Mundy (John
Clewley): 97 • Reuters/Claudia Daut: 8, 30, 80 • Reuters/Rickey Rogers: 62 • Reuters/
Stringer: 40 • Pietro Scozzari: 16, 58 • David Simson: 3, 4, 10, 12, 17, 29, 42, 61, 69, 74,
87, 108, 113, 120, 123, 124, 127 • Jenhor Siow: 130, 131 • Tan Chung Lee: 9, 32, 41, 70
• Liba Taylor: 14, 19, 26, 36, 44, 47, 48, 71, 73, 78, 81, 83, 115, 117, 118, 121

PRECEDING PAGE

Cuban students wave their national flag.

Marshall Cavendish Benchmark
99 White Plains Road
Tarrytown, NY 10591
Website: www.marshallcavendish.us

Originated and designed by Times Editions
An imprint of Marshall Cavendish International (Asia) Private Limited
A member of Times Publishing Limited

Library of Congress Cataloging-in-Publication Data
Sheehan, Sean, 1951-
    Cuba / by Sean Sheehan. – 2nd ed.
        p. cm. – (Cultures of the world)
    Summary: "Explores the geography, history, government, economy, people,
        and culture of Cuba" – Provided by publisher.
    Includes bibliographical references and index.
    ISBN 0-7614-1965-9
    ISBN 9780-7614-1965-5
    1. Cuba – Juvenile literature. I. Title. II. Series: Cultures of the world (2nd ed.)
    F1758.5.S54 2005
    972.91 — dc22   2005009362

Printed in China

7 6 5 4 3 2

CONTENTS

Cuban teens and street graffiti.

A Cuban flag, a portrait of
Fidel Castro, and various
notices share space on a
shop wall.

INTRODUCTION

DEPENDING ON ONE'S POINT OF VIEW, Cuba is either the last bastion of communist evil in the Western Hemisphere or the world's greatest hope for social equity and environmentally sensitive development. Cuban history and geography have conspired to put this Caribbean nation at the center of global politics since Fidel Castro waged a successful revolution against poverty and inequality over 40 years ago.

Today Cubans enjoy one of the best standards of education and health care in the developing world. Cuban art and music are vibrant symbols of the country's past and present. Cuba's natural environment is unsurpassed in the Caribbean. Cuban warmth and humor, along with miles of sun-drenched beaches, attract millions of visitors. At the same time, Cubans live with a tightly controlled economy and are not free to oppose their government. The continued animosity between Castro and the U.S. government impacts nearly every aspect of Cuban life.

GEOGRAPHY

CUBA IS THE WORLD'S seventh-largest island and is the largest of the Caribbean Islands. The islands are the visible summit of a submerged mountain range that once joined North America and South America. Cuba is 750 miles (1,207 km) long and ranges in width from 25 to 120 miles (40 to 193 km). It lies 90 miles south of Florida and 90 miles east of Mexico's Yucatán Peninsula. Cuba is slightly smaller than the state of Pennsylvania.

TOPOGRAPHY

The island of Cuba itself makes up just under 95 percent of the national territory. There is also the Isla de la Juventud, or Isle of Youth, near the southwestern coast and some 1,600 islets, most of them uninhabited.

Above: **The peak of Gran Piedra, a distinctive feature of the Sierra Maestra.**

Opposite: **A river runs near Santiago de Cuba. Cuba has almost 600 rivers.**

MOUNTAINS The island of Cuba consists mostly of flatlands and rolling plains, but mountains in the west and east and across Cuba cover almost a quarter of the total land mass.

The largest mountain range, the Sierra Maestra, is 155 miles (249 km) long and contains the highest peak at Pico Turquino (6,578 feet, 2,005 m). Another striking feature of the Sierra Maestra is Gran Piedra (Huge Rock), which is dominated by a sheer rock face that stretches to its summit at 3,936 feet (1,200 m). The central mountain range includes the Sierra de Trinidad. Here summits rarely exceed 4,000 feet (1,220 m), so roads and railway lines have been built across these mountains, linking the southern shore with the northern coastline. The Sierra de los Órganos in the west is the lowest of the three main ranges, never exceeding 2,500 feet (762 m) and containing limestone caves.

A STUDY IN CONTRAST: TWO CUBAN ISLANDS

The Isla de la Juventud, or Isle of Youth *(right)*, is Cuba's largest offshore island. It has a total area of 850 square miles (2,200 square km) and is situated 60 miles (97 km) south of the mainland. It used to be the destination for many students who came to study in Cuba, and for that reason, the name of the island was changed from Isle of Pines to Isle of Youth in 1978. In the past, the physical isolation of the island made it a suitable site for incarcerating political prisoners. In 1931 a maximum-security prison, based on the plans for a similar prison in Joliet, Illinois, was opened. Fidel Castro is the Isle of Youth's most famous former prisoner, and the prison is a prime tourist attraction. Only the north side of the island is

developed, while most of the southern side is undeveloped woodland and swampland, mostly inhabited by fishermen and their families.

Another of the lightly inhabited Cuban islands is Cayo Largo. It is 15 miles (24 km) long and up to 5 miles (8 km) wide. The island is situated 87 miles (140 km) southeast of the Isle of Youth. Geographically, it is little more than a strip of sand in the ocean, and its entire southern coast is one long beach. As such, it has been entirely given over to tourism. The only Cubans allowed on the island are those working in the tourist industry. The majority of visitors tend to be affluent Europeans and Canadians seeking the sun and sand of the Caribbean. Tourism is one of Cuba's main industries and main source of foreign exchange.

CLIMATE

The climate in Cuba is temperate and semitropical. Trade winds that blow westward across the island produce a moderating influence on the weather. Cuba's dry season lasts from November to April and the wet season from May through October. The average minimum temperature is 73°F (23°C) and the average maximum is 82°F (28°C). Temperatures occasionally exceed 100°F (38°F) in the summer, and during the winter, freezing temperatures are sometimes recorded in the high mountain areas.

Rainfall is generally moderate with three-quarters of the annual precipitation occurring during the wet season. The average annual rainfall is 52 inches (132 cm). While some years are characterized by drought, others receive very heavy rainfall. Both weather extremes have wreaked havoc in Cuba and on its peoples' lives.

Cuba lies in an area that experiences fierce tropical hurricanes. On average, one hurricane every two years will hit Cuba usually during the wet season, especially from September to October. Typically, a hurricane has winds of over 160 miles (257 km) an hour and dumps 12 inches (30 cm) of rain in a period of 24 hours, causing extensive damage. In 1963 Hurricane Flora killed over 7,000 people in Cuba and Haiti.

The semitropical Cuban climate supports year-round vegetation in all parts of the island.

WATERWAYS

"This island is the most beautiful I have seen, full of very good harbors and deep rivers, and it appears that there is no tide because the grass on the beach reaches almost to the water, which does not usually happen when there are high tides or rough seas."

—Christopher Columbus, describing Cuba in October 1492

Nearly 600 rivers in Cuba, mostly short and unnavigable, ensure that the land is well-irrigated and suitable for agriculture. The two longest rivers are the Zaza, in central Cuba, and the Cauto, in eastern Cuba, north of the Sierra Maestra mountain range.

The largest and most interesting lake in Cuba is the Laguna de la Leche (Milky Lagoon), which is located near Cuba's northern coast. Since a number of channels connect the lagoon with the sea, tidal movements disturb the calcium carbonate deposits that form the floor of the lagoon and give rise to its milky appearance.

Crocodiles and alligators live along the coastal marshes and within the labyrinth of small rivers. There are large enclosed zones where thousands of these animals are farmed for their meat and their hides.

Cuba has many natural ports. The important ones include Cienfuegos, Havana, and Santiago de Cuba.

The banana frog, the smallest amphibian in the world, is found in Cuba.

FLORA AND FAUNA

Cuba's isolation from other land masses or other islands has resulted in the development of unusually small species of fauna unique to Cuba. The banana frog, and the tiniest mammal in the world, the almiqui, are both found in Cuba. The nocturnal almiqui, or Cuban *Solenodon*, is an endangered shrew-like creature with long claws for catching insects. The smallest scorpion in the world can also be encountered in Cuba, which is less than a 10th of an inch long. Another minuscule creature is the *Polymita* genus of land snail, only found in the northeast of Cuba and believed by the early Afro-Cubans to have magical powers.

None of the 14 species of snakes inhabiting the island are poisonous, although one of them, the boa, kills by suffocating its prey by constriction and can grow to 13 feet (4 m) in length.

Nearly 400 species of birds have been recorded on the island, including the bee hummingbird, the smallest in the world. Because it measures only 2 inches (5 cm), including the bill and tail, it is often confused with an insect. One of the most eye-catching of the island's birds is the Cuban *Trogon*, a member of the Trogonidae family, which is made up of 35 species. These birds inhabit the tropical forests of the Americas, Africa, and Asia. The Cuban Trogon is about the size of a small crow and its feathers are metallic green with bright patches of black, red, and white. It enjoys special status as Cuba's national bird because it has the colors of the Cuban flag.

Butterflies and moths contribute to the kaleidoscope of color that characterizes the flora and fauna of Cuba. There are more than 180 species of butterflies, and of these nearly 30 are found only in Cuba. Their colorful displays can be imagined when they bear such names as Orange Sulphur, Mosaic, and Cuban Buff Zebra.

The Cuban Trogon

FLOWERS AND TREES GALORE

Some 22 percent of Cuba's land is covered by forests and woods, so not surprisingly there are a tremendous assortment of trees and flowers. Among the largest are the flame trees *(below)* and the African tulip trees that provide shade during the heat of the day and advertise their presence with grand lily-like blooms. The frangipani, whose flowers are used for garlands, is common. Cuba's national flower is the butterfly jasmine, which has white flowers that look like butterflies. The climate encourages a colorful mixture of flowers to flourish. A typically eye-catching assortment around a home in the countryside may include pink or white congea climbing the walls and bougainvilleas of magenta, mauve, red, and orange crowding the path to the door.

The value of Cuban wood was appreciated by the Spanish, who used it to build their fleet of ships transporting treasure across the Atlantic. Today there is commercial value in the sale of mahogany, ebony, oak, and teak. The bark of mahogany is also used to treat ailments, including rheumatism and pneumonia. Cuba has more than 60 species of palm trees, including the stately royal palm, Cuba's national tree, which grows to over 75 feet (23 m) tall. The versatile tamarind tree, usually found lining roads, bears fruit pods used as a flavoring, preservative, and medicine, besides being a commercially valuable timber. Along the coastline grow almond, mangrove, and wild fig trees. Cuba's rarest tree is the cork palm, regarded as a living fossil because it has existed since the Cretaceous Period 100 million years ago.

LIFE IN THE WATER

With some 900 different species of fish to be found around Cuba, it is not surprising that the island attracts tourists who like to fish. American writer Ernest Hemingway, who lived in Cuba for a number of years, was an enthusiast of game fishing. The chance to catch a marlin, one of the fastest-swimming fish in the world, still draws tourists. There are various prestigious international fishing tournaments in Cuba, including the Hemingway Marlin Fishing Tournament begun by the writer in 1950. Many local competitions engage the talents of Cubans.

The distinctively marked clown fish is found in Cuban waters.

The warm waters surrounding Cuba are home to a myriad collection of fish, including clown fish, queen angelfish, tangs, and blue striped grunts. On the surface, turtles swim placidly and share the water with dolphins and porpoises, while above them flying fish open their pectoral fins and scull the water with their tails to gain momentum. Underwater, the colorful fish life and impressive coral reefs can be appreciated with little more equipment than a pair of goggles. Certain areas of Cuban waters have been classified as biosphere reserves by UNESCO (United Nations Educational, Scientific and Cultural Organization).

Some of the fish to be found in Cuban waters are best appreciated from a safe distance. These include moray eels, which grow up to 5 feet (1.5 m) long and have sharp teeth that discourage divers from getting too close. Equally voracious predators are the barracudas, whose fang-like teeth have injured bathers and divers.

Most of Cuba's nonsugar manufacturing is located in and around Havana, making it the busiest and largest city on the island.

HAVANA

Three out of four people in Cuba live in the urban areas. The largest city is the capital, Havana, located in the northwest of the main island. It has a population of over 2 million, or about 18 percent of the total Cuban population of 11.3 million.

In the 16th century Havana became an important Spanish outpost in the Caribbean. For over 500 years the city has witnessed poverty and wealth and one rule after another. One of the most built-up areas in the capital, Habana Vieja (Old Havana), is the old colonial city. Situated on the shores of Havana Bay, Old Havana contains a number of buildings of outstanding architectural interest that date back to the period of Spanish colonization. In 1982 UNESCO listed Old Havana as a world heritage city. Efforts are being made to restore many of these buildings. To accommodate the growing urban population, new housing has been built in the suburbs, creating small new townships.

OTHER CITIES

The largest city after Havana is Santiago de Cuba, which is situated on the southeastern end of the island, scenically located overlooking a bay and nestled by the foothills of the Sierra Maestra Mountains. Around 550,000 people live there, many of whom are Cubans working at the U.S. naval base at Guantánamo Bay less than 100 miles (161 km) away. Santiago de Cuba has an international airport and one of the country's busiest ports. Other sources of employment are provided by numerous factories near the city, an oil refinery, and power stations. It is a very cosmopolitan city, due partly to the mix of African and Spanish heritages.

The high price of importing petroleum products limits motorized transportation in Cuba, even in its capital city, Havana.

Santiago de Cuba, founded by the Spanish as the country's capital, is today known as the "Capital of the Revolution" because of its historical association with the overthrow of Fulgencio Batista's dictatorship. It was here in 1953 that a small group of rebels launched a surprise attack on the Moncada Barracks, an event regarded as a pivotal moment in Cuba's modern history.

The next most important city is Camagüey, situated in the center of Camagüey Province between Havana and Santiago de Cuba. This province is one of Cuba's most prosperous regions, mainly due to its agriculture and livestock. Cubans identify the city with the production of *tinajones* (teen-a-HOHN-ays), clay urns 10 feet (3 m) wide and 5 feet (1.5 m) tall. Traditionally these were placed outside houses and often buried up to half their height in the ground for the storage of cool water. Although they are no longer used for this purpose, their presence outside buildings in Camugüey is a characteristic sight.

HISTORY

CUBA'S STRATEGIC LOCATION IN THE Caribbean at the mouth of the Gulf of Mexico has played an important part in the island's history. The Spanish used Cuba's natural harbors as ports for ships plying between the New World and Spain. In the 20th century, Cuba's proximity to the United States made its internal politics and foreign relations with Communist countries particularly significant.

Throughout Cuba's history, a pattern of tensions between major players has been repeated: Spanish conquerors and settlers versus indigenous inhabitants; Spanish-born versus Cuban-born; landowners versus poor farmers; and more recently, the United States versus Cuba.

EARLY INHABITANTS

Cuba's earliest known inhabitants were the Ciboney and Guanahatabey, who lived in the western half of the island. The more numerous Taíno arrived much later, around A.D. 1200. Evidence of cave-dwelling peoples dates back to 3500 B.C. These include pictographs of magical signs.

The Taíno were closely related to the Arawaks of South America, and the two groups are often spoken of as one people. It is very likely that these early settlers on Cuba were descendants of agriculturalists who had migrated north from the Amazon Basin of South America.

Opposite: **The National Theater building in Havana bears a Spanish architectural style.**

Below: **Taíno Indians lived in *bohío*, or farmer dwellings, like these, which are still seen in the rural and mountain areas of Cuba. The roof thatch is made of palm leaves or grasses and the walls are usually of palm wood.**

CONQUERING THE TAÍNO

The Taíno lived in village communities varying in size from a few families to a few thousand people. Each community had a leader. They raised such crops as potatoes and manioc, grew yams and other vegetables, and caught fish and birds to eat. They wove cotton, cultivated the tobacco plant, and produced their own stone tools. Little is known about their religious beliefs, but idols were carved out of stone, wood, and clay.

The peaceful culture of the Taíno was ill-suited to meet the challenge of Spanish invaders, who first landed on the island with Christopher Columbus on October 27, 1492. In later years more Spanish arrived, and they had little trouble subduing the Indians. The Taíno were forced into servitude. Those who resisted were killed. A missionary who accompanied the Spanish described how the Spanish repaid the hospitality of the Taíno by raping women and killing entire village populations. Children starved to death when parents were rounded up to work in mines.

The actual settlement of Cuba by Spain began in 1511. By then, other Caribbean islands had been settled. The leader of a community in Hispaniola, Chief Hatuey, fled to Cuba with his surviving followers. He tried to convince the Cuban Taíno to resist the invaders, but they mistrusted him. Hatuey went into hiding, joined by some Taíno, and when the Spanish arrived, he led his followers in guerrilla warfare against the Spanish. But Taíno arrows were no match for horses and gunpowder, and their ambushes only delayed the inevitable. Hatuey was captured and, when he refused to reveal the location of his people, burned at the stake. Within a very short time the Taíno faced extinction. They died fighting the invaders, from disease, from overwork in mines, and on plantations controlled by the Spanish.

SPANISH RULE

In 1511 Diego Velázquez de Cuéllar arrived to establish a permanent settlement at Baracoa. The Spanish came to Cuba looking for gold. Taíno panned the rivers and dug mines, and when more labor was needed slaves from Africa were shipped to the island. When Cuba's yield of gold was found to be poor, the Spanish turned elsewhere. In 1519 a large expedition that included some 3,000 Indians left Cuba under the command of Hernán Cortés, lured by tales of riches, to the Aztec Empire in Mexico. The African slaves were left on the island with the remaining Taíno Indians, to work on plantations in a system known as *encomienda* (ayn-koh-mee-AYN-da)—work in return for "protection" and conversion to Catholicism.

The remainder of the 16th century witnessed the decline and final elimination of the Taíno population. Black slaves became more important on plantations, although the development of Cuba's real wealth—sugar and tobacco—was slow. More and more Spanish ships stopped at Cuba in transatlantic crossings, laden with plunder from Mexico and Central and South America. The Spanish developed the harbor at Havana, and toward the end of the 16th century they built Morro Castle at the harbor entrance, signifying Cuba's newfound importance.

Above: **The Spanish built Havana's Morro Castle, protection against pirates, between 1589 and 1630. The lighthouse at the entrance was added in 1844.**

Opposite: **Taíno Indians panning and mining for gold under the watchful eyes of the Spanish.**

Cuba still has a few remaining gauchos, or cowboys. Cuba's central plains were ideal pastures for cattle ranching. By the end of the 18th century, however, much grazing land was given over to the cultivation of the more profitable sugarcane.

CUBA BECOMES IMPORTANT It was well into the 18th century before the Spanish settlement in Cuba showed commercial success. Ships brought thousands of new slaves as sugar and tobacco became more profitable due to increased European demand and the opening of trade with the Spanish colonies and North America. Havana emerged as the obvious capital of the island as the harbor developed its own shipbuilding industry to complement its role as a major naval base.

As Havana became sufficiently important, it gained the attention of the British, who occupied the harbor and town in 1762 and stayed there for nearly a year before the Spanish regained control. By 1774 a census showed that the population had reached over 170,000, consisting of 44,000 blacks, 96,000 whites, and 31,000 people of mixed parentage.

During the decades that followed, the population swelled with thousands of French colonists who fled neighboring Haiti seeking refuge from an uprising of Haitians. In 1801 Haiti invaded the eastern part of Hispaniola, and the Spanish colonists who had controlled part of the island also fled to Cuba. Two years later, when France sold Louisiana to the United States, more European colonials came to an increasingly prosperous Cuba. By the first decade of the 19th century, Cuba was economically self-sufficient and no longer depended on cash subsidies from Spain.

REVOLT AGAINST SPAIN

Long before slavery was abolished in Cuba in 1886, the population of Cuba was further mixed by the arrival of indentured Chinese laborers. The island's economy was booming, due chiefly to the sugar industry, and Cuba needed an alternative source of labor because of growing incidents of uprisings by black slaves. A focus of discontent at the time was the perception by Cuban-born Spanish known as *criollos* (kree-OH-yohs), or Creoles, that they were being discriminated against in favor of the *peninsulares* (pay-neen-soo-LAR-rays), or Spanish born people living in Cuba. The government in Spain handed power and privileges to the *peninsulares*.

By the mid-19th century, *peninsulares* and *criollos* clashed frequently in the pursuit of opposite aims. The *peninsulares* were mainly military personnel, government representatives, landowners, and slave-owners who preferred Spanish rule. The *criollos* included teachers, professionals, and writers, some of whom owned slaves. The *criollos* were divided, one group wanting independence from Spain but maintaining slavery, the other freedom for everyone in Cuba.

Meanwhile, the United States was becoming increasingly interested in Cuba's economy and politics. Its offers to buy the island from Spain were officially rejected while attracting support within the business community on the island. Among the rebels watched closely by Cuba's powerful northern neighbor were Carlos Manuel de Céspedes, Antonio Maceo Grajales, and the best-loved and remembered of Cuban patriots, José Martí.

Cuban rebel leader Antonio Maceo was nicknamed Bronze Titan for his courage and strength.

"CUBA LIBRE!" (FREE CUBA)

The first major revolt, known as the Ten Years' War (1868–78), actually started with El Grito de Yara (The Cry of Yara). Yara was a town near the plantation of Carlos Manuel de Céspedes, a wealthy lawyer. He freed his slaves and proclaimed (the 'cry') the independence of Cuba from Spain. Toward the end of the war, Spanish soldiers ambushed and shot Manuel.

The uneasy peace concluded in 1878 at the Convention of Zanjón did not solve the central issue of Cuba's status of independence. Spain was willing to liberalize its colonial rule, but calls for independence or incorporation into the United States were not answered. The inconclusive Ten Years' War left approximately 50,000 Cubans and 208,000 Spanish dead.

Antonio Maceo, known to Cubans as the Bronze Titan, joined the rebels and contributed greatly to their guerrilla tactics. When not ambushing the Spanish, he read widely and organized the rebels' living quarters, including hospitals and food stores, with the help of his mother and wife. After the Ten Years' War, he left for Jamaica with his family and continued the revolutionary struggle from abroad. There he met José Martí *(above)*, whom many call the Apostle of Freedom.

A war of independence erupted again in 1895, with both sides showing a grim determination to resolve the conflict through violence. The rebels were led by José Martí, whose rallying call was *"Cuba Libre."* Within three years Spain controlled only the coastal towns.

Martí was convinced of the need for Cuba to develop as an independent country. When only 16 he was sentenced to hard labor in a stone quarry, imprisoned on the Isle of Pines (later known as Isla de la Juventud, or Isle of Youth), then banished to Spain because of his political opinions. In Spain he graduated with a law degree in 1874, and his revolutionary fervor expressed itself in poetry and prose. Banned from Cuba, Marti traveled to the United States where he campaigned relentlessly for an independent Cuba. He established the Cuban Revolutionary Party in New York and sought to enlist the aid of the U.S. government, but it was not prepared to help him officially. In 1895 he organized an armed force that landed in Cuba. Thousands of Cubans died in the rebellion that followed, including José Martí, who was killed during an encounter with troops loyal to the Spanish government. The best-loved leader of the Cuban revolution died when he was only 42. Many statues have been erected in his memory. Generally less well-known is the fact that he wrote the verses of the famous song *Guantanamera (A Girl from Guantanamo)* and that he was the grandfather of actor César Romero, who played The Joker in the 1960s *Batman* television series.

U.S. RULE

At first, the United States remained officially neutral during the tumultuous events in Cuba, though secretly negotiating with Spain to purchase the island. U.S. business companies, by then the dominant investors in Cuba's sugar industry, called for U.S. intervention in Cuba to protect their interests. Then in February 1898, an event occurred that caused the United States to enter the war to free Cuba from Spain.

The battleship USS *Maine* was sent to Havana with the ostensible mission of helping to evacuate U.S. citizens endangered by the fighting between Cuban revolutionaries and loyalist forces. When the ship exploded in the harbor in February 1898, under circumstances that have never been fully explained, the United States blamed Spain and declared war on the country. This was the start of the Spanish-American War, which was one-sided and brief because Spain was unprepared for military engagement in its colony.

With U.S. troops as well as nationalist rebels fighting against the loyalist troops, the war came to an end in August 1898. In December 1898, under the Treaty of Paris, Spain relinquished its claim to the island. A U.S. military government was set up to govern the island.

For three years following the Treaty of Paris, U.S. army general Leonard Wood governed Cuba. The army mainly worked on public works programs, such as the building of schools and roads, in order to facilitate U.S. economic and cultural development of Cuba.

Although the United States brought order to the war-torn island, many Cubans believed they had changed one undesirable master for another. There was also a sense of bitterness that, through one single incident, the revolutionaries had been denied the glory of winning a war that had lasted decades and cost so many Cuban lives.

In 1881 Cuban physician Carlos Finlay first proposed the view that the deadly disease yellow fever was carried by mosquitoes. U.S. army doctors investigated the claim, and in 1900 they were able to confirm it. A mosquito control program led to the disease's subsequent eradication.

SELF-RULE?

To satisfy Cuban nationalism, the U.S. administration helped draw up a new constitution in 1901 that granted Cuba a degree of self-rule in 1902. But Afro-Cubans were denied the vote, and the Platt Amendment (authored by Senator Orville Hitchcock Platt), which the United States insisted had to be part of the constitution, established the right of the United States to intervene in the island's affairs. The amendment also gave the United States the right to buy or lease land for naval bases. Accordingly, in 1903, a permanent lease on Guantánamo Bay was granted to the United States. The naval base is still in operation today.

CORRUPTION

From 1906 to 1910 U.S. troops returned to the island because of frequent uprisings against government leaders who were more interested in accumulating power and personal wealth than in the people's welfare. During the 1920s a dramatic rise in the price of sugar brought prosperity, but because U.S. companies owned most of the profitable concerns, many Cubans were denied the fruits of economic success.

When the Great Depression in the 1930s worsened the already bad conditions, the regime of President Gerardo Machado was seriously threatened. In 1933 an army sergeant, Fulgencio Batista, organized a coup against Machado. Batista had U.S. support and became Cuba's next leader.

BATISTA'S DICTATORSHIP

Fulgencio Batista (1901–73) (*right*) ruled as commander in chief of the armed forces from 1934 to 1939. He was elected president in 1940. He governed Cuba well and made improvements to the infrastructure.

The constitution allowed a president to serve only one four-year term in office. In 1952, however, Batista staged a second coup and ruled as Cuba's dictator before being deposed himself in 1959. Commerce became brisk because of the government's repression of trade unions. Foreign companies set up businesses in Cuba and exported their profits. This time round Batista apportioned little money for public works, as large-scale corruption permeated every aspect of political life. Havana became the playground of the wealthy with its profusion of casinos, bars, and brothels. The tourists who filled Havana's casinos were oblivious to the poverty underpinning the private wealth of a minority of politicians and their close supporters. In the rural areas especially, many families could barely feed themselves, and it was common to see malnourished children.

CASTRO'S REVOLUTION

The young lawyer Fidel Castro had planned to contest the 1952 elections, but when these never took place he adopted more direct action. On July 26, 1953, he led a small group in an attack on the Moncada Army Barracks in Santiago de Cuba. The rebellion failed, and Castro was imprisoned.

After his release in 1955, Castro went to Mexico to plan a second attempt at overthrowing the Batista dictatorship. A close colleague at this stage was the famous Argentinian revolutionary, Che Guevara. In December 1956 Castro, Che Guevara, and about 80 others landed in eastern Cuba. Most of the group were killed or captured, but 12 men, including Castro and Guevara, hid in the Sierra Maestra.

Over the next two years an increasingly successful guerrilla campaign was conducted against the government. The initial group of 12 was joined by supporters who shared their vision of freedom. The rebels gained the support of ordinary Cubans.

Elections were organized for November 3, 1958. Batista's chosen supporter was elected president, but it meant little. Soon after, the army deserted Batista, who fled Cuba on January 1, 1959. The rebel army marched into Havana on January 8, and a new era in Cuba's history began.

Opposite: Images of Ernesto (Che) Guevara, Fidel Castro's close revolutionary partner, are everywhere in Cuba. The nickname *Che* (chay) is Argentinian for "Hey, man!", and Guevara loved using the word in his speeches. Devoted to revolutionary causes, he inspired Fidel Castro to a similar dedication that led Castro to support revolutions in other parts of Latin America.

A billboard proclaims defiance at the United States: "We're not scared of you, Mr. Imperialist."

FRICTION WITH THE UNITED STATES

The downfall of Batista's repressive government was hailed as a triumphant victory both in Cuba and around the world. The corruption and inequality that characterized Batista's Cuba had long been known. Over the next couple of years, however, relations between Cuba and the United States deteriorated. By January 1961 diplomatic relations between the two countries were formally broken.

The rupture was caused by Castro's determination to build a revolutionary new society based on socialism. Cuba lowered rents by half and put industries under state control. The principal losers were U.S. companies or individuals who owned these enterprises and buildings. U.S.-owned sugar estates and cattle ranches were taken over from 1959 to 1960, then oil refineries were seized. It is estimated that $1 billion in U.S.-owned properties were expropriated by the Cuban government. As a result, the U.S. government imposed a trade embargo against Cuba in October 1960. All remaining U.S. assets were then seized by the Cuban government.

Cuban refugees poured into the United States after the downfall of the Batista government. They included officials of the Batista government, those involved in corruption and vice, and ordinary Cuban citizens opposed to Castro. Many of the exiles formed an underground movement to plan the invasion of Cuba. In late 1959 some exiles launched sporadic firebomb attacks. Though not officially sanctioned by the United States, these attacks used U.S. planes and ammunition. The attacks increased tension between the two countries.

In February 1960 Cuba and the Soviet Union signed their first trade agreement. As Russian trade and assistance grew, the U.S. government became increasingly concerned by Castro's leftist leanings. In 1961 the United States supported an attempt by Cuban exiles opposed to Castro to invade the island at the Bay of Pigs.

Pg 29: **The Soviet embassy building still stands prominently in Havana, but the alliance between Cuba and Russia has weakened since the end of the cold war in 1991.**

Below: **The Soviet tank that Fidel Castro rode in during the Bay of Pigs incident is on display outside the Museo de la Revolución in Havana.**

THE BAY OF PIGS INCIDENT

The aim of Operation Pluto, the secret name of the invasion planned by the exiles with help from the U.S. CIA, was to train 1,500 Cuban exiles, arm them, and help them land on Cuba, where Cubans were expected to welcome their "liberators."

It started with the bombing of two Cuban airfields on April 15, 1961, which killed seven and wounded 44. The U.S. planes used were marked with the Cuban military insignia, to give the illusion of a military uprising. Rumors of the landing alerted the Cuban authorities, who rounded up anti-government suspects, including foreign journalists and CIA agents.

The invasion force landed on April 17 in the Bay of Pigs at Playa Giron. Within 48 hours, the invaders were captured. The incident increased Castro's popularity, especially since he was seen in action, organizing troops at Playa Giron. About 120 men were killed in the confrontation, and nearly 1,200 captured. The leaders were returned to the United States in exchange for cash, and the rest in exchange for medicine and food.

THE CUBAN MISSILE CRISIS OF 1962

In 1962 the world came perilously close to a nuclear war. As Cuba became more isolated by the hostility of the United States, it increasingly turned to the Soviet Union for support. The Soviet Union responded to Cuba's request for military assistance to reduce the risk of another U.S.-backed invasion like the abortive Bay of Pigs incident.

In the summer of 1962 U.S. spy planes gathered photographic evidence of Soviet missile installations in Cuba (*below*). The United States felt threatened because the missiles had a range of 1,000 miles (1,609 km), and Soviet jet bombers, also in Cuba, were capable of carrying nuclear weapons. On October 22, 1962, President John F. Kennedy warned his country of the threat from a nuclear attack and demanded that the Soviet Union dismantle the sites. He made it clear that not dismantling the missile sites would be viewed as a hostile act justifying nuclear retaliation by the United States.

The United States put a naval blockade around Cuba to halt further shipments of arms. On October 28, 1962, Soviet premier Nikita Khrushchev confirmed the missiles would be removed from Cuba if the United States promised not to invade the island. The offer was accepted and war was averted.

The Cuban missile crisis was seen as a confrontation between two world powers. Fidel Castro was angry that he was not consulted before Khrushchev's decision, which he disagreed with, but he did not have the power to act.

MISSILE TRANSPORTERS
12 PROB GUIDELINE MISSILES
HEAVY EQUIPMENT
5 MISSILE DOLLIES
20' LONG CYLINDRICAL TANKS
MISSILE TRANSPORTERS
OPEN STORAGE

RECENT HISTORY

During the height of the cold war between the United States and the Soviet Union, Cuba openly supported a variety of socialist regimes. Cubans fought in Angola, Ethiopia, and Nicaragua. This deepened U.S. hostility toward Castro. Since the collapse of the Soviet Union in 1991, Cuba no longer has the capacity to arm or fight for other regimes, but the U.S. government continues to tighten the trade embargo in order to loosen Castro's hold on power.

In 1996 the United States enacted the Cuban Liberty and Democratic Solidarity Act, also known as the Helms-Burton Act. This law prohibits any foreign company that does business in the United States from trading with or in Cuba. The act has been widely resisted by the European Union, Canada, and Mexico.

In 2004 U.S. president George W. Bush restricted cash remittances from Cubans in the United States to their relatives in Cuba. Castro retaliated by revoking the 1993 law that permitted Cubans to hold U.S. dollars and imposed a 10 percent surcharge on dollar conversions to Cuban pesos.

Cuba is not viewed by most of the world as a rogue state or a threat. This means that U.S. sanctions, while inconvenient for Cubans and Cuban-Americans, do not have enough international support to damage Castro. Indeed, some argue that they bolster his popularity by strengthening Cuban nationalism.

GOVERNMENT

CUBA'S SYSTEM OF GOVERNMENT is defined in its constitution as "a socialist state of workers and peasants, and all other manual and intellectual workers." Political power is exercised through the Cuban Communist Party, and Cuba is one of the few countries in the world still committed to the revolutionary ideologies of Karl Marx and Vladimir Ilyich Lenin. The average Cuban pays little attention to the ideas of these long-dead political thinkers, but Fidel Castro's influence remains paramount and the loyalty he inspires is extraordinary.

CONSTITUTION

The constitution was amended in 2002 to cement the permanence of the country's socialist system. This was in response to Cuban dissident Osvaldo Paya's Project Varela, which had gathered the signatures of over 11,000 Cubans on a petition for greater political and economic freedoms.

The president is the head of state, leader of the government, and the commander of the armed forces. The Council of State issues laws in the form of decrees and is made up of the president (Castro), six vice-presidents, a secretary, and 23 other members. The Council of Ministers—the president, vice-presidents, and ministers—is the chief administrative organ with executive power.

Above: **The Capitoleo was built to resemble the U.S. Capital building in Washington, D.C.**

Opposite: **Castro and Venezuelan president Hugo Chavez in Havana in 2004.**

THE NATIONAL ASSEMBLY

The Presidential Palace now houses the Museo de la Revolución.

The 609-member National Assembly is elected directly by universal suffrage. Candidates are nominated at meetings with a number of work organizations, including the armed forces and student groups. The election for the National Assembly held in 1993 was the first election in which citizens went to the polls and voted in secret.

Seventy-five percent of the members of the National Assembly are Communist Party members. There are no legal opposition parties so candidates either run as Communists or as independents. All elected government officials, including members of the National Assembly, are elected to five-year terms. Efforts by dissidents to have Cubans protest by spoiling their ballots have been largely unsuccessful.

The members of the Supreme Court, Council of State, and Council of Ministers, including the president, are chosen by the National Assembly. The Assembly re-elected Fidel Castro as head of government in March 2003. The National Assembly also selects members of the judicial arm of the government.

THE COMMUNIST PARTY

The 1976 constitution guarantees that the Communist Party shall remain the only legitimate party in Cuba. An amendment in 2002 made one-party Communist rule irreversible. As such, the party is the most important political institution in the country.

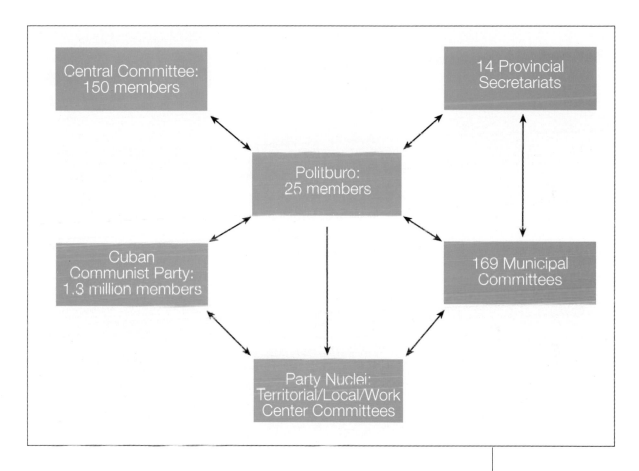

The structure of the party is similar to that of the government. There is a Central Committee of 150 deputies elected at party congresses. Deputies elect members of the Politburo who form a ruling body.

A party congress is held approximately every five years. The first was held in Havana in 1975. These are opportunities for delegates of the party from all over the island to convene to discuss reforms and future plans. At the time of the fall of the Soviet Union in 1991, Castro affirmed Cuba's future as a communist country. He allowed limited foreign investment and economic reforms. These were reaffirmed in the last party congress held in October 1997.

Ever since the party was established in 1965, it has been controlled by Fidel Castro and his brother Raúl. At the 1997 party congress, Castro named his brother as his successor as president.

The Cuban Communist Party structure and membership.

LOCAL GOVERNMENT

The country is divided into 14 provinces that form the basis for the administrative and political organs of power. From east to west, they are Guantánamo, Santiago de Cuba, Holguín, Granma, Las Tunas, Camagüey, Ciego de Avila, Sancti Spiritus, Villa Clara, Cienfuegos, Matanzas, La Habana, the City of Havana, and Pinar del Río. There are 169 municipalities; one, the Isle of Youth, is a special division.

Local government is based around provincial and municipal assemblies. Members of municipal assemblies are elected to terms of two-and-a-half years, and each municipal assembly is headed by an executive committee.

Cuban students pass by a poster in Havana for the 40th anniversary of the revolution in 1999.

The Cuban police force is divided into principal, municipal, and neighborhood divisions.

Members of these executive committees form the provincial assemblies.

Another important organization of local administration is known as the Committee for the Defense of the Revolution. The neighborhood bodies that form this organization are the most local form of government. The name of the organization goes back to the early days of the revolution when an invasion from the United States was a very real threat and surveillance groups were established to counter it.

FIDEL CASTRO

Fidel Castro was born in 1926, the son of a sugar plantation owner from Spain. He was an exceptional athlete in high school. In 1945 he entered the University of Havana, where he received a Ph.D. in law.

He joined the Cuban People's Party, named Ortodoxos, after graduating from Harvard in 1950. On his second attempt, he overthrew the Batista government and declared the Cuban Revolution a success. Castro has been consistently underestimated throughout his career as the longest-serving leader in the world. Contrary to expectations, he did not become a typical tin-pot dictator. In fact, he has prohibited a cult of personality to form in Cuba. As a result, there is not one statue of Castro on the whole island and no evidence he has enriched himself. Castro also prefers to keep his private life undisclosed. Most Cubans know little about his family and have hardly seen pictures of his family members in the media.

Castro has survived numerous attempts on his life and continues to exude strength and stamina in public engagements. He appears to be a remarkably eloquent and cheerful individual. His ability to talk at length

INTERVIEWS WITH CASTRO

Since 1959 Castro has given many interviews to newspaper, radio, and television journalists. His views have become particularly interesting because, while many countries have abandoned Communism as an economic and political system, Cuba has steadfastly refused to compromise its basic principles. The following are responses given by Castro since 1991.

On the collapse of the Soviet Union: "All of this points to what a slur it was to say that Cuba was a satellite of the Soviet Union. We have proven that we were not because, although the Soviet Union has disappeared, we have continued to struggle, we continue to pursue our own revolutionary path, we have not become discouraged, we have not surrendered, and we are confronting this harsh test with full confidence in our future."

On the 1993 elections for the National Assembly: "What other country under the siege and blockade that we face, would have the courage to call elections, a free secret ballot where people can vote yes or no, during a period akin to war? Would your country [Britain], with Hitler on the French coast ready to invade, have called such an election?"

On what will happen after the death of Castro: "I don't think that socialism can be identified with me personally. I didn't invent it."

On the United States: "I have never failed to recognize the merits of the American people. One should not forget that the United States was a colony that fought hard for its independence."

On the U.S. Declaration of Independence: "It's really very beautiful. I've always had a great liking and admiration for Abraham Lincoln. The Declaration stated that all men are created free and equal. But at the same time, slavery was maintained for nearly 100 years after that, which goes to show that the formal statements of principle do not always correspond with the facts."

On the number of assassination attempts made on his life: "If there were an Olympic event in this field, I would certainly have won the gold medal."

On why he wears a guerrilla uniform: "These are my clothes, I've worn them all my life, they are comfortable and simple, they cost little, they never go out of style. But excuse me if I ask you a question: When you interviewed the Pope, did you ask him why he always wears that white outfit?"

Castro's remarkable charisma is evidenced by the number of names he has acquired over the years, including El Comandante (koh-man-DAN-tay)—The Commander, El Caballo (ka-BUY-yoh)—The Horse, and El Jefe (HAY-fay)—The Chief. He is sometimes referred to as just El, and ordinary Cubans call him Fidel even though they may never have met or spoken to him.

is legendary. During the 1960s and 1970s it was common for him to deliver a speech of three or four hours. In 1969 he spoke on television for seven hours non-stop!

HOW FREE IS CUBA?

On the plus side, Cubans support the system that has provided them a standard of health, education, and cultural enrichment that is superior to the majority of Latin American and Caribbean countries. The government has reduced the gap between rich and poor so that when there are hard times, everyone suffers together. It is not a perfectly equal society but everyone is educated, has access to medical care, and has his or her basic needs guaranteed.

On the minus side, the Castro government has refused to accept the need for political opposition. Underground groups of dissidents exist and are subject to sudden arrest and imprisonment. The number of political prisoners is not known. Past attempts by the United States to destabilize Cuba gives the government a reason for feeling paranoid and an excuse for harassing those who are committed to peaceful political change.

There is a tension in Cuba between those who remember life under Batista and U.S. influence and the younger generations who only know the difficulties of living in Cuba. Older people tend to support the revolution and Castro because they fear a return to grinding poverty, inequality, and ignorance. Younger Cubans are divided between believing their elders and supporting the revolution, and wanting to see changes in the way things are done. They would like to have the right to disagree with the government and express themselves through alternative political parties. Some want Castro to step down. Most want a more open economy; very few want to return to pre-revolution society.

BACK TO THE FUTURE?

The anti-Castro Cuban American National Foundation, a very effective pressure group of Cuban exiles in Miami, has detailed plans for running

Cuba's prisons, like many prisons in other countries in the region, do not provide sufficient food and adequate medical care to its inmates.

a post-Castro government. The Foundation points out that many U.S. corporations are ready to fuel what is seen as an instant $2 billion market. Cuba is widely regarded as the last undeveloped business market in the Western hemisphere.

Those loyal to Castro claim that business interests would return Cuba to a state of economic dependence on the United States. Most Cubans, even those critical of Castro's authoritarian regime, do not wish to see Cuba become a U.S. colony again.

Cuba is finding its way without Soviet support, but there is considerable speculation about what will happen when Castro dies. He has appointed his brother Raúl to take his place, but Raúl himself is not a young man. Only time will tell the fate of the Cuban revolution after Fidel.

Posters exhort Cubans to be alert and vigilant. The ability of ordinary Cubans to stoically accept material deprivation has impressed people visiting the island.

GUINNESS
WORLD RECORDS

CERTIFICATE

Jose Castelar Cairo and h
rolled the world's lar
14.86 m (48.7

GUINNESS

ECONOMY

THE CUBAN ECONOMY HAS NEVER been able to satisfy the needs of its population for a number of reasons involving foreign interests and domestic decisions. At the root of the problem is an over-reliance on sugarcane and its derivatives for export earnings.

Before the revolution, Cuba was a major sugar producer and tourist destination. Visitors, primarily from the United States, came to the island for its casinos and nightlife. Most of the lucrative businesses were foreign-owned, including sugar estates and refineries. Many Cubans worked for low wages, suffered poor health, and received little, if any, education.

After the revolution, public education, health care, and mandated minimum wages vastly improved the lot of poor Cubans. The government expropriated foreign business holdings, including U.S.-owned sugar estates and casinos. The United States imposed a trade embargo on Cuba in the hope of crippling the new government. The Soviet Union filled the void and offered Soviet petroleum for Cuban sugar, which prompted Cuba to grow even more sugarcane. With the collapse of the Soviet Union, this support disappeared.

Sugar remains an important Cuban commodity today, but tourism is increasingly becoming a major revenue generator for the country.

Opposite: **On February 25, 2005, Cuban cigar-maker Jose Castelar Cairo attempts to break his own world record for making the longest cigar. Castelar won Guinness World Records for rolling cigars measuring 35 feet (11 m) and 45 feet (14 m) in 2000 and 2003, respectively.**

Below: **A resort hotel in Viñales. Tourism in Cuba brings in badly needed foreign currency.**

A worker puts finishing touches on cigars in a cigar factory in the city of Trinidad, in central Cuba.

NATURAL RESOURCES

Cuba is fortunate because it is the largest country in the Caribbean, and most of its land is low, flat, and fertile. As the primary resource of this comparatively small country, land ownership is vital to economic well-being. After the revolution, the government expropriated foreign-owned estates and set upper limits on how much land a single owner could control. It also distributed land to former agricultural laborers so that they received rights to land they had farmed for generations.

The primary crop is sugar. It used to be grown on large estates retained by the government, which was about 75 percent of all agricultural land. As part of the agricultural reform in 1993, these estates were broken into smaller units and leased permanently and for free to cooperative work groups. These cooperative farms, or Basic Units of Cooperative Production, are required to produce quotas of essential crops. Once those quotas are fulfilled, they can grow any crops they like and sell them. The cooperatives get to keep the profits from these sales.

MAIN CROPS

Sugar is still king, but other crops are grown in larger quantities now, especially rice, corn, and cassava. Tobacco is also grown to make cigarettes for local consumption and high-quality cigars for export. Coffee is grown mostly in the east of the island. With the absence of imported pharmaceutical drugs, Cubans have turned to growing many medicinal plants. Livestock mainly consists of cattle, chickens, and pigs.

OTHER RESOURCES

Since 1959 Cuba has expanded its fishing industry with subsidies from the Soviet Union. The industry was heavily affected by the Soviet Union's collapse but has since picked up momentum. Major exports include lobsters, shrimp, and fish.

Like other Caribbean islands, Cuba is not particularly mineral-rich, but it has more than 10 percent of the world's known nickel reserves. Nickel is the second-largest export item after sugar.

SUGAR IS NOT ALWAYS SWEET

Sugar production has long functioned as the backbone of Cuba's economy, and until 1991 the export of sugar to the Soviet Union and Eastern Europe accounted for over 75 percent of the island's revenue from trade. Cuba's imports were worth $8 billion because of the favorable price the Soviet bloc was prepared to pay. Today Cuba can only sell its sugar at world market prices, and the result has been a forced reduction of imports.

Since the days of Spanish rule the Cuban economy has been locked into the sugarcane industry. For a long time the industry's high level of profitability was linked to the easy availability of cheap hired labor. After the departure of the Spanish, Cuban farmers became independent owners of sugar farms. Too soon, however, U.S. corporations moved in. When the price of sugar reached an all-time low in the early 1920s, large U.S. companies were able to take over near-bankrupt farms, smaller corporations, and sugar mills. By 1930 nearly three-quarters of Cuba's sugar industry was owned by U.S. corporations, and the plantation worker found that the European colonial master had been swapped for one nearer home.

Another problem that continues to bedevil the Cuban sugar industry—whether under Spanish, U.S., or Cuban control—is the unpredictability of drought. A lack of expected rain can seriously damage the value of the eventual sugar harvest.

INDUSTRY

In the decade following the 1959 revolution, the entire industrial and manufacturing sector was nationalized. The largest industries are food processing, pharmaceuticals, petroleum, and cement. Sugar milling is the chief form of food processing, allowing for the production not only of raw sugar but also such byproducts as brandy, rum, and molasses.

Even before the collapse of Cuba's main trading partners in Eastern Europe, the government was trying to diversify the country's manufacturing base and reduce its dependence on sugar. Fluctuations in world prices for sugar, combined with the adverse effects of a drought, led economic planners to actively seek new sources of industrial employment.

Approximately 25 percent of the labor force is employed in the industrial sector. This figure would be a lot higher if Cuba had a larger international market for its exports and the basic energy supplies needed to fuel activities in these sectors.

CUBAN PRODUCTS Apart from natural resources, there is great potential to expand exports of processed and manufactured goods. For example, Cuban rum has gained a following around the world for its quality. Cuba is expanding its biotechnology industry and exports its products to more than 40 countries worldwide. These products generate about $100 million in revenue annually.

An oil rig in Cuba. The country is constantly searching for new energy sources to power its growing industrial base.

Animal power replaces Soviet-built farm machinery that has fallen into disuse for lack of spare parts.

THE BIG SQUEEZE

The United States first imposed trade restrictions on Cuba in 1960, a year after Castro took power. By 1963 these were extended to include a full embargo on trade and the prohibition of all dollar transactions with Cuba.

About 30 years later, new restrictions were proposed. The Cuban Democracy Act of 1992, sponsored by Congressman Robert Torricelli, tightened economic sanctions against Cuba in an attempt to weaken Castro and hasten his downfall. Following that came the 1996 Helms-Burton Act, which extended the trade ban to all foreign companies doing business in the United States.

The embargo was relaxed slightly in 2000, allowing U.S. food companies to sell to Cuba. In a very unpopular move in 2004, President George W. Bush capped remittances of money to Cuba from Cubans living in the United States. Observers claim that these were efforts to bankrupt Cuba of precious foreign currency reserves. The United States has maintained that it will only relax restrictions when Cuba releases its political prisoners and when there are free presidential elections in the country.

The international community has largely stopped observing the embargo, leaving the United States isolated in this regard. Tourists from Canada and the European Union flock to Cuba, and their companies and governments invest, buy, and sell there. The UN General Assembly voted against the embargo for 13 consecutive years. U.S. actions run counter to international opinion as expressed by the United Nations and such trade bodies as the World Trade Organization (WTO), but so far there have been no binding decisions to force the United States to back down. The saddest consequence of the embargo has been that ordinary Cubans often lack basic goods, such as medicine and food.

Cuban workers load Russian ships in Havana port in January 1989. With the breakup of the Soviet Union, the economic situation has changed drastically.

SOCIALISM OR DEATH

Some observers argue that the embargo has given Castro justification for his periodic crackdowns on free speech and dissident activity. Castro claims he is head of a state under siege and cannot tolerate dissent. He often questions whether any other country in the world would be "free" when the world's largest superpower, lying 90 miles (145 km) off the coast, had repeatedly asserted its hostility. He stirs up nationalist fervor with his slogans and is quite possibly more popular today than ever because he continues to resist U.S. pressure. The international community has been vocal in its condemnation of Castro's human rights abuses. However, they have not committed to the embargo, arguing that if has not worked in over 40 years, it is unlikely to start working now.

Besides sun-and-sea attractions, Cuba boasts such sites as the El Bar del Medio in Old Havana, one of Ernest Hemingway's favorite haunts. Hemingway was a legendary 20th-century American writer.

EL TIEMPO ESPECIAL

Following Soviet collapse in 1991, Cuba faced a sudden shortage of food, petroleum, and equipment. The threat of starvation and an increase in poverty were very real. Cuba entered *el Tiempo Especial* (ayl tee-AYM-poh ay-spay-see-al), or the Special Period, a sort of economic martial law introduced by Castro. Strict rationing was implemented to ensure that what goods were available were fairly distributed. A number of reforms were initiated to reduce the degree of dependency on imported goods.

Cuba also changed its food production in a way that attracted much attention for its success and novel techniques. Faced with a sudden loss of the chemicals and machinery supplied by the Soviet Union, Cuba worked hard to grow its own food without using much pesticides, fertilizer, or machinery. Large tracts of land, most of which were previously used to grow sugarcane and tobacco for export to the Soviet Union, were parceled out and used to grow other crops that met Cubans' food needs.

In 1993 new legislation allowed citizens to hold and spend U.S. dollars in a bid to save the economy after the Soviet collapse. This encouraged the currency, tourism, and remittance businesses. By the late 1990s money remitted to Cuba from abroad became the backbone of Cuba's income.

TOURISM—AGAIN!

Before 1959 Cuba's second biggest source of revenue was tourism. The island was infamous for its casinos and dubious nightlife and was a convenient vacation spot for wealthy North Americans. After the revolution all tourist hotels and casinos were closed, and U.S. citizens were not allowed by their government to visit the island. The tourism industry did not recover until the mid-1970s when Canadians, Latin Americans, and Europeans—especially from Spain—were attracted to the beautiful island that was far less expensive than most of its Caribbean neighbors. Since the late 1980s, increasing the number of visitors has become a national priority.

Cuba is being marketed as an ecologically friendly island with plenty of natural attractions. In the 1992 Earth Summit in Rio de Janeiro, Castro publicly asserted Cuba's favorable attitude toward its environment. Many natural areas have been preserved in Cuba, and with the incentive of tourist revenue, the country is committed to protecting them in the future.

Cuba's tourist capital is Varadero, but there are also many other destinations competing for the nearly 2 million visitors that arrive each year. The growth of the tourism industry has been phenomenal. In 2004 tourism accounted for 41 percent of foreign exhange income in Cuba, compared to just 4 percent in 1990. Canadian tourists accounted for the bulk of the 2004 arrivals, followed by Italian, French, German, and Spanish tourists. To maximize foreign currency earnings, vacationers are required to use euros and currencies other than the U.S. dollar for all their expenses while on the island.

The legislation was repealed after 10 years in an effort to reduce Cuba's dependence on U.S. dollars.

On the international scene Cuba sought investment from abroad and changed its laws to allow foreigners to once again own Cuban land or businesses. The main investors in joint ventures are from Spain, Canada, and Italy. Cuba's other trade partners include the Netherlands, France, Mexico, Venezuela, China, and Russia. These joint ventures have revitalized industry, created jobs, and pumped much-needed foreign currency into the battered Cuban economy. Most of the investments have been directed at the expanding tourism market, which is the largest foreign exchange earner in Cuba. There are also other innovative partnerships, which include a joint venture to turn Cuba's natural gas byproducts into electricity and a partnership with a European company to market Cuban tobacco.

While Cuba is still too dependent on sugar, domestic creativity and hard work coupled with international partnerships are helping the country to get stronger.

ENVIRONMENT

OF ALL THE ISLANDS in the Caribbean, Cuba has the best chance to preserve its remaining animals, plants, and ecosystems. Government initiatives begun in the 1990s have deepened the Cuban commitment to a healthy and sustainable environment. Previously Cuba suffered through a long period of poor environmental awareness that resulted in a damaged environment.

DEPLETION OF NATURAL RESOURCES

Under Spanish and British colonization, massive clearing of land was undertaken to make way for sugar cultivation. Sugar continued to be central to the Cuban economy during U.S. rule, Batista's regime, and the post-revolution government. This long period of monoculture resulted in deforestation. When Columbus landed in 1492, 95 percent of the island was forested. The forest area declined to 50 percent by 1900, and by 1959 it dipped to 13 percent. The government then implemented reforestation projects to counter this decline, and in 2004 about 22 percent of Cuba was forested.

With help from the Soviet Union, Cuba built one of the most modern sugar industries in the Caribbean. Sugarcane fields were scientifically managed using fertilizers, pesticides, and herbicides, and as much of the work as possible was done using machinery. Unfortunately these chemicals, along with the discharge from sugar refineries, contaminated waterways in Cuba. The deforested land was eroded by wind and rain that washed the soil into rivers and the sea, contributing to water pollution. Hurricanes caused more erosion, increasing salinization, and reducing the fertility of the soil. Cuba's many marine treasures were damaged by overfishing.

Above: **Large-scale clearing of land took place in Cuba in the first half of the 20th century to make way for sugarcane cultivation.**

Opposite: **Beautiful scenery can be enjoyed in Cuba's nature spots, such as at Laguna del Tesoro in Zapata Peninsula.**

51

Exhaust fumes from ve-
hicles such as this truck
add to the pollution in
Cuban cities.

Coastal cities had little in the way of pollution control for vehicle exhaust fumes and poor solid sewage disposal management. Industrial cities, such as Havana, were highly polluted.

ENVIRONMENTAL AWAKENING

In a speech at the 1992 Earth Summit in Rio de Janeiro, Castro proposed that since the cold war had ended, the resources that developed countries used to accumulate arms would be better spent on fighting ecological destruction. Environmental laws and projects in Cuba increased after this speech, and Cuba became more conservationally aware as a result of government policies and political circumstances.

After the collapse of the Soviet Union, Cuba faced a shortage of petroleum and its byproducts fertilizers and pesticides. Farmers were forced to adopt organic methods, such as using animal dung and plant waste as fertilizers. Instead of chemical pesticides, farmers used integrated pest management strategies that included intercropping (growing two or more species together), crop rotation (growing different crops in succession), and relying on natural insecticides (birds, predatory insects, and plant extracts).

To address the acute shortage of food during the Special Period, as much space as possible was fully utilized for agricultural production. Even residents in cities, such as Havana and Cienfuegos, took up gardening, because they were required to produce their own fruit and vegetables. They, too, were legally required to use organic methods to protect people and the environment from chemical toxins.

Machines that ran on gasoline could no longer be used, so people everywhere adopted greener alternatives. Oxen were put back in the

The shortage of petroleum that followed the Soviet collapse led Cubans to turn to greener alternatives for transportation, such as bicycles

fields, donkeys took over the highways, and bicycles filled urban streets. To meet the need for soil and fertilizer, Cuban engineers began to work on projects to recycle sewage from cities. In short, Cuba became a large-scale experiment in green living.

Cuba has since come through the worst of the crisis due to increased tourism, agricultural diversification and innovation, and a variety of trade deals with countries that do not observe the U.S. embargo. Official policy continues to promote green living because it saves the country from having to import fuel and expensive chemical products. Cubans also realize that part of the attraction for the millions of visitors to the island is its natural beauty, lower levels of pollution, and pristine natural areas.

The Caribbean reef squid is one the many creatures populating Cuban waters.

RICH BIODIVERSITY

In addition to government backing at the highest level, Cuba benefits from a host of scientists, biologists, and other trained professionals who are able to address the environmental issues in the country.

Cuba is also naturally blessed with a rich species biodiversity. The country was once a land bridge between the continents of North America and South America, so the number of animal and plant species is high. Island ecosystems in the region are unique in ways biologists are still trying to understand.

Cuba has set aside 263 protected natural areas, which range from highland forests to coastal mangroves and inland swamps. There are six important wetlands and a number of World Heritage Sites, so designated for their natural significance.

Coastal mangroves and inland swamps are among the many protected natural areas in Cuba.

Cuba has beautiful beaches and is a major tourist destination.

ASSESSMENT

Cuba has accomplished environmental miracles, in part because of its forced isolation from typical large-scale investment and in part because of a government commitment to sound environmental management. Cuba has justly earned world praise for its achievements in this area, but some argue that there is still more to be done.

Many parks and reserves are well-conserved because the government tightly controls business activities. This means that people are not allowed to use or abuse the parks for commercial gain without permission. It also means that the parks will survive only as long as the government can enforce its will. A more successful strategy would tie people's interests to natural areas so that they become active participants in conservation. Given Cuba's position as a major tourist destination, one of the easiest and most logical steps would be to promote ecotourism. Those who earn a living from this business would be motivated to care for the attractions that tourists pay to see. The government is considering ecotourism, but so far it has been more concerned with maintaining its tight control on private enterprise than with getting Cubans directly involved in conservation.

There is much reason to be hopeful that Cuba will continue to defend its natural areas and work toward greener living strategies in the future. It serves as a model for what can be done in both urban and rural areas with the right planning, organization, and know-how. If the government could find a way to forge a deep commitment to these practices among Cubans by making them part of a healthy economy, Cuba will remain the Caribbean's premier natural wonder.

THE IVORY-BILLED WOODPECKER—DEAD OR ALIVE?

Deep in the forests of eastern Cuba, there is a slim chance that a bird thought to be extinct may still exist. The ivory-billed woodpecker, which is about 18 inches (46 cm) long and has a wingspan of 3 feet (0.9 m). It is black, red, and white and has a distinctive ivory-colored beak.

This species of woodpecker was once found throughout old growth swamps in Cuba and the southern United States, but since it requires large tracts of mature forest, it did not fare well in the face of logging and clearing of its habitat. The last confirmed sighting in the United States was in 1951. The bird was believed to be extinct, but then was sighted in Cuba in 1986. Bird-watchers are hopeful that this beautiful bird has survived, and they regularly mount expeditions into the swamps in the hopes of seeing one. The sighting prompted the Cuban government to protect the forest where it was seen, and this area later grew into the 300-square-mile (777-square-km) Alexander von Humboldt National Park in eastern Cuba.

Although the ivory-billed woodpecker has not been sighted for a few decades, Alexander von Humboldt National Park is the bird's best chance for survival on the planet as it contains untouched ecosystems and forests. Here, pine forest grows to the edge of coastal mangroves, and a full 30 percent of Cuba's native plant species thrive.

CUBANS

CUBANS ARE A MIXTURE OF RACES. Underlying their ethnic differences are similarities in temperament that help characterize the Cubans as a nation. They have a reputation for being friendly and sociable. They have a strong sense of national and patriotic pride in the achievements of the last half-century, as they have overcome the odds to survive as an independent country.

ETHNIC MIX

More than half of the population consists of Cubans of mixed African and European descent. They are classified as mulattoes. Cubans who are of European, mostly Spanish, descent are classified as Creoles. A significant proportion of Cubans are blacks, descended directly from slaves brought from West Africa in the 19th century. The Chinese are a minority. They were brought to Cuba in the 19th century when the African slave trade was coming to an end.

Above: **An easy camaraderie exists among these Cuban children in a neighborhood playground.**

Marriage between blacks and Chinese used to be forbidden, but today all of the different races intermarry. This accounts for the surprising variety in skin tones found among the Cuban people.

More recent immigrants to Cuba are political refugees from Latin America. Castro has always championed socialist revolutions in South America and offered a home to dissidents who have had to flee their own countries. After the overthrow of socialist president Salvador Allende of Chile in 1973, for example, many Chileans fled to Cuba.

Opposite: **A light-skinned Cuban family. Whites and mulattoes make up 88 percent of the population in Cuba.**

A group of teenagers in Havana.

RACIAL PREJUDICE

An important part of Cuba's identity as a socialist state is that everyone has equal rights and opportunities. In most areas of life, egalitarian principles are seen to be successfully operating. Very little racism is seen in personal relationships and, in this respect, Cuba has made tremendous progress. Racist attitudes do, however, still influence some aspects of Cuban life, and black Cubans are not always treated in the same way as Cubans of European descent.

The higher ranks of many occupations are more likely to be filled by people of European or mixed European descent. This tendency is apparent in the tourist industry, where white Cubans are more likely to be employed as receptionists, tour guides, and waiters. Black Cubans are much more likely to be employed as hotel housekeeping staff or laundry operators. Discrimination also seems to operate in the government departments that run the education system and the armed forces.

Young black Cubans are the most disaffected group of citizens. They suffer the same material deprivations as everyone else, but they often claim to be harassed by the authorities because of their color. The police are accused of being biased when it comes to dealing with young blacks suspected of being involved in criminal activity.

Racist attitudes that do persist in Cuba are a legacy of the past. Before 1959 racism was an accepted fact that pervaded all areas of Cuban life. Blacks occupied lower paying jobs, and racial segregation existed in social life. It was not uncommon for mulatto parents to prevent their children from marrying black people in the hope that this would improve their social and economic opportunities. During U.S. rule, black and white Cubans were not encouraged to mix with each other.

Despite Cuba's claim to equality, lighter-skinned Cubans still have an advantage over their darker counterparts in some sectors of the job market.

THE ETHNIC MELTING POT

The proportion of different peoples in Cuba is:

51 percent	Mulattoes of mixed European and African descent
37 percent	Whites of European descent
11 percent	Blacks of African descent
1 percent	Asians of Chinese descent

Six-year-old Elian Gonza-lez smiles while playing soccer in the backyard of his relative's home in Miami in 2000.

CUBANS ABROAD

Before 1959, when grinding poverty was a way of life for many Cubans, the United States beckoned as a paradise. Most Cubans who could afford the expense and secure entry left for Miami. When the Batista dictatorship collapsed in 1959 the people who fled the island were affluent Cubans who realized their privileged lifestyle would not be tolerated by the new socialist regime. The majority of this exodus of about 200,000 people went to the United States. Florida was the most popular destination, and here they formed the basis for a community of Cuban exiles. Other Cubans settled in Mexico and various South American countries.

In 1965 Castro allowed disenchanted Cubans not of military age to leave. Over the next eight years another 300,000 Cubans left for the United States. Very few Cubans left their country after this. In 1980, however, some 125,000 Cubans were ferried from Mariel in Pinar del Río to Miami. U.S. president Jimmy Carter welcomed them as political refugees. Some of these refugees later returned to Cuba.

THE FLORIDA CONNECTION

There are Cuban communities in New York, Chicago, and Los Angeles, but Miami is the U.S. city with the largest population of Cuban-Americans. Their numbers are increasing as more refugees make the 90 mile (145-km) journey from Cuba. Sometimes they arrive more dramatically than in small boats and rafts. In 1992 a Cuban plane was hijacked by its own pilot, with some support from the passengers, and landed in Miami.

Some Cuban refugees, especially those from the post-revolution exodus after 1959, have settled down as permanent Cuban-Americans. Many of them were professionals in Cuba and found it relatively easy to establish a new life in the United States. Their children have never been to Cuba. Many of the 1.2 million Cubans who have settled in the United States since 1960 are sometimes viewed as reluctant immigrants. However, polls of Cuban-Americans asked whether they wished to return permanently to Cuba provide conflicting conclusions. A 1991 poll by Florida International University found that about 23 percent said they would return if the government changed to a democratic one. The same poll also found that there was an increasing sense of frustration that political changes did not seem likely to happen anytime soon in Cuba.

Most Cuban-Americans who are politically active campaign for the overthrow of the Castro regime. They represent an influential lobby group with the U.S. government that wants the United States to finance an invasion so that they can reclaim the property they abandoned or that was confiscated by the regime in 1959.

Since the early 1990s the number of those escaping from Cuba in small boats and rafts across the Straits of Florida has increased steadily. Brothers to the Rescue are volunteer pilots, mostly Cuban-Americans, who fly regularly over the Straits of Florida in search of refugees. The refugees are accepted as political asylum seekers and put in touch with friends or relatives in the United States. In 1999 a 6-year-old boy, Elian Gonzalez, was found floating in an inner tube in the Florida straits. He was one of three Cuban refugees who survived when the boat they took to escape to the United States capsized. Elian's mother was one of those who died on the journey. His relatives in Miami took him in and pleaded with the authorities to let him stay in the United States. Other Cuban-Americans joined in the campaign, but in the end the boy was returned to his father in Cuba.

The United States has given Cubans special treatment because they are seeking asylum from a political regime viewed as repressive. By contrast, refugees from other Latin American or Caribbean countries are categorized as fleeing deplorable conditions in impoverished economies.

Children in Cuba wait patiently as their mothers chat.

DEMOGRAPHY

Demographic trends reflect the changing economic and social conditions of Cubans. In the years immediately after 1959, the birth rate rose steadily in response to improvements in the standard of living. This was especially the case among low income groups. However, the death rate also increased because a large proportion of doctors left the country. The U.S. trade embargo also resulted in a serious shortage of medicines.

The mortality rate gradually dropped as standards of health improved and new doctors were trained. With greater economic stability, education for women, and a greater chance of infant survival, the birth rate also dropped to 12 per 1,000 people in 2004. This averages out to approximately 1.7 children per woman. The infant mortality rate is slightly lower in Cuba than it is in the United States at 6.5 deaths per 1,000 live births. Cubans now enjoy long healthy lives with a life expectancy of 75 years for men and 79 years for women.

NATURAL FLAIR

Traditional Cuban dress is colorful and flamboyant. There is no national costume, but whenever Cubans dress up they do so with an innate sense of style and exuberance. It may also be a reflection of their sense of pride. The subtropical climate encourages the wearing of light cotton clothes. An open-necked shirt, often worn over cotton slacks, is the typical male dress. Women tend to wear form-fitting and colorful clothes. These are usually short-sleeved or sleeveless, appropriate to the climate.

The item of dress that comes closest to being labelled a national costume is the *guayabera* (gwuy-a-BAY-ra), a long-sleeved cotton top that is a cross between a shirt and a light jacket. It usually has four pockets on the front.

The *guayabera* was originally a form of male dress dating back to the 18th century. A Spanish tailor in the village of Yayabo, in Sancti Spiritus Province, is said to have first promoted its use. It is claimed that the word Yayabo accounts for the name *guayabera*. Women add embroidery, as well as buttons and tucks, to the *guayabera*, and it is now worn by Cubans of both sexes.

LIFESTYLE

IN SPITE OF THE CURRENT austerity measures Cubans have a lively and fascinating lifestyle. The role of the state is central to many areas of life, but the value of individuality continually asserts itself. The country's ideology stresses duty and communal effort, but the ordinary Cuban has a healthy disrespect for too much authority. Enjoying oneself is still a national hobby. Lifestyles have had to adapt to harsh economic conditions, but adjustments are often made with imagination, good humor, and a sense of optimism.

Above: **Cubans wait in line at a shop. Cuban shops often do not display signs advertising the type of goods or services offered.**

Opposite: **A Cuban family living in a village sits on steps with their pet dog.**

ECONOMIC SYSTEM

Many aspects of life are managed in Cuba in a way that is quite different from the United States and most other countries of the world. Until the early 1990s Cuba shared many similarities with Eastern Europe and the Soviet Union. With the economic changes in Eastern Europe, the predominant role of the government in Cuban life now has parallels in only a few other places, such as China and Vietnam.

Cuba has a mixed economy with a combination of private enterprise and state-controlled businesses. State enterprises run in tandem with the private sector, which makes up for deficiencies in what the state can produce or import. While the state system still runs on rationing and centralized distribution of goods, the private system is based on cash and barter exchanges. This favors those who have access to money and goods sent from relatives abroad or obtained through contact with foreigners. Many tourists know how this works and bring extra toiletries, clothes, or medicines to leave as tips for hotel workers and guides. In the private economy there are still many regulations about what can be sold and at what price. These regulations ensure that everyone in Cuba is able to afford basic necessities.

LINES Long lines are a feature of life in Cuba, especially for subsidized services or products. People wait in line not only for meat and bread, but also for bus and train tickets, ice cream, or a new shipment of television sets. The easygoing nature of Cubans means that most lines develop haphazardly and new arrivals simply ask *L'ultimo?* (LOOL-tee-moh)—or *L'ultima?* (LOOL-tee-ma) if addressing a woman—to establish whether they have correctly identified the last person in the line. When the line is for a basic food item in very short supply the needy consumers are more disciplined and regulated. Some people wait a long time to be near the front of a line and then sell their position to someone just arriving. Young unemployed Cubans earn some money by hiring themselves out to wait in a line for those who have money but little patience.

Once a common sight in Havana, old 1950s American cars are becoming rarer as they consume too much precious fuel.

TRANSPORTATION The severe shortages of gasoline in the early 1990s are now over but with the high price of oil worldwide, Cubans still restrict their use of cars. In the countryside, donkeys and horses are a common sight, and in the cities, people ride bicycles and walk when they can.

MICROBRIGADES

Before 1959 poverty and deprivation were widespread in Cuba. Housing was inadequate and overcrowded, especially in cities. In the post-revolution years an increase in the birth rate focused attention on the need for drastic improvements in the provision of housing. Cuba responded by forming microbrigades.

Microbrigades are small groups of workers who take time off from their usual occupations to assist with building programs. The workers are a mixture of professional and manual workers of both sexes. The general plan is that a section of the workforce, from a factory or government department, is mobilized to construct five-story blocks of apartments under the supervision of building professionals, while the remaining workforce maintains production levels.

In urban areas microbrigades are most likely to be engaged in public housing programs, though the focus has now shifted to tourist development and other projects. In the countryside the building brigades are involved in building new schools or homes for the elderly.

The use of these building brigades serves political and practical purposes. Cuba is intent on constructing the kind of society where all the citizens see it as their duty to contribute to the public good.

CUBAN HOMES

One positive side to Cuba's central development planning is that there are no homeless people in the country. All housing projects are initiated by the state, but tenants are able to purchase their homes through installment payments. Many Cubans become owners of their homes that way. Owners of larger houses are allowed to rent out sections as apartments. Hardly anyone lives alone in Cuba, so houses and apartments are nearly always built as family homes.

The Spanish style is clearly visible in such cities as Havana and Trinidad, where many 19th century buildings are still standing. Residents in some of the older, Spanish-style buildings are forbidden from making changes to the original structures. Preserving a building's architectural integrity is not, however, the main reason for withholding improvements. Many older houses in the cities are crumbling and suffering from a lack of amenities, but there is not enough money to finance the repairs.

The style of old colonial buildings finds an echo in the traditional style of many rural homes. Balconies and patios are a common feature of houses in both Spain and the Caribbean. The architecture is a natural response to a hospitable climate that encourages people to think of their home as extending beyond the four walls of the house itself. People like to relax at home; sitting on a patio with friends or neighbors comes naturally to Cubans.

Men retire at the age of 60 and women at 55. The social security program collapsed with the Soviet breakup, and the amount of pension retirees receive is about half the average monthly wage. Retirees save money on rent because they often share their homes with their children, especially if the children are unmarried. Nevertheless, some items are scarce, and if available, they are usually too costly for a retiree to buy. By 2025 a quarter of Cuba's population is expected to consist of people over the age of 60.

Opposite: **Colonial buildings In Old Havana are ornately styled.**

Below: **These spacious buildings with well-kept surroundings are located at the waterfront in Cienfuegos Bay.**

A WOMAN'S LIFE

The Cuban government has earnestly tackled discrimination against women. It is illegal to discriminate against women in any field of employment, including the armed forces. Husbands of working women are legally bound to share the housework and child rearing, although in practice this does not always happen. Rape is not commonly reported in the press, and certain types of rape carry a death penalty. The legislation designed to achieve equality for women is included in the country's consitution and the Family Code of 1975. This act also includes laws for pregnant women, such as extra rations and 18 weeks of maternity leave.

In some industries, such as this clothing factory, women still represent the majority of workers.

EQUALITY ON THE BATTLEFIELD

Castro has often acknowledged that without the help of women in building and maintaining the underground organization supporting the guerrillas in the 1950s, the revolution would never have succeeded. Celia Sanchez, who became his aide in the closing years of the war, was waiting on the beach in 1956 with transport and supplies of gasoline when Castro and his followers landed from the yacht *Granma*.

Children in school are reminded of the many women who played crucial roles in Cuba's struggles, including Lidia Doce and Clodomira Acosta, who were tortured to death by Batista's men and thrown into the sea. In September 1958 the first all-woman combat platoon, Mariana Grajales, was formed. Platoon member Teté Puebla became the highest-ranking woman officer in the Revolutionary Armed Forces.

Women fought at the Bay of Pigs and some lost their lives there.

Women have a strong presence in the country's workforce, making up about 44 percent of the total. This is possible mainly because the state provides childcare facilities for mothers. Centers of employment usually have day nurseries, allowing infants to be looked after during working hours. Especially in the fields of law, academia, and medicine, women have attained the kind of professional success that is more commonly associated with men in most other countries.

While legislation of equality for women helps in some respects, it takes a long time to overcome cultural biases. Management positions and government appointments are predominantly held by men. Some women employees feel that they stand lower chances of being promoted because they are undervalued by their employers. Yet others feel burdened by domestic duties and do not have the time to upgrade themselves by attending training. In general, however, women in Cuba suffer much less discrimination than women in other countries in the region.

MARRIAGE

Older Cubans remember the days when girls of marriageable age went out only when chaperoned by an older brother or relative. Courting began in the local park where girls would walk around in pairs, with arms linked around each other's waists. The boys would stroll around some distance away. Courtship was highly formal, subject to parental approval, and expected to culminate in a marriage ceremony at the local church.

During the first 10 years after the revolution the number of marriages doubled, while the rate of divorce increased eightfold. These dramatic increases reflected the radical changes affecting women and men. Improvements in economic conditions, such as the lowering of rents, increased people's purchasing power and encouraged the planning of families. The traditional role of women as homemakers was challenged

MACHISMO

While in theory Cuba is committed to sexual equality, there is still a strong macho element in the national culture. In the machismo ethic, the female role is primarily domestic and submissive to male authority. The male role is to exercise authority and display macho aggression in both private and professional life. In other words, while men are encouraged to exhibit machismo, women are expected to conform to opposite values of virtue and demureness.

The regulation that says it is a man's duty to share household chores is part of a process designed to eliminate machismo. An article of the Family Code, entitled "Rights and Duties Between Husband and Wife," is recited by the person officiating at the marriage ceremony. In addition, children are educated in a highly political way that includes an emphasis on sexual equality. Traditional attitudes die hard, however, and many Cuban males would be upset to think that whistling or hissing at a female was anything more than a charming compliment. People joke that adultery is a national sport—for men only.

A complicated aspect of Cuban machismo, arising perhaps from its roots in family values, is that it is not something simply imposed by males on females. A joke in a Cuban magazine for girls sums up the paradox. "Your boyfriend is terribly macho," says a girl to her friend. "Yes," replies the other, "Aren't I lucky!" Cuban men will readily admit to their cultivation of machismo. However, behind the flirting and the showing off, men respect women.

as more and more women entered the workforce and benefited from equal educational opportunities. The role of religion declined, and the government established "Palaces of Marriages" across the country where secular marriage ceremonies were conducted. Divorce laws were liberalized, and the process of obtaining a divorce became readily available to all social classes. Divorce is easy and continues to be fairly common. Cuba has one of the highest divorce rates in the world, with 3.4 divorces for every 1,000 people. The United States has a higher rate of about 4.2. Among the reasons cited for the prevalence of divorce in Cuba are economic difficulties, increased economic responsibility for women as they join the workforce, and having to live with other family members in the same house. Cohabitation is a common occurrence. Birth control is widely practiced and abortions are relatively easy to obtain.

EDUCATION FOR ALL

Education, from nursery school to university, is free for all Cubans. School transportation, textbooks, equipment, and school meals are all provided free by the state. Cuba has the highest per capita teaching staff in the world, at one teacher for every 36.8 Cubans. In 2004 the government committed to the goal of having one teacher for every 20 students in a bid to improve education even further. Cuba has only 2 percent of Latin America's total population, but it produces 11 percent of the region's scientists.

Illiteracy has been virtually eliminated. Over a million adults were taught to read and write in a literacy campaign that began three years after the revolution. Adult education remains an important part of the national system of education. There are branches of the main universities in all the provinces, and many areas have schools of music, art, and ballet. These facts represent one of the country's greatest achievements, and Cubans feel justly proud of their educational resources.

The most commonly seen school uniform is khaki or blue trousers or skirt, white shirt or blouse, and a red neckerchief. Due to the favorable climate it is quite common for classes to be conducted outdoors.

Schools were adversely affected by the Soviet collapse because the supply of textbooks, paper, and school equipment became scarce. Now Cuba has forged ties with other countries willing to trade with it, but it often has to pay a higher price. Nevertheless, education is one of the bedrocks of the revolution and continues to be a priority, whatever the cost.

Coeducation is the norm in Cuba.

HOW IT WORKS

Cubans must attend school between the ages of 6 and 15. The first level is primary school, which lasts six years. Then they move on to basic secondary, which lasts three years. After that they have a number of choices: quit school, continue with technical or professional training, or prepare for university. The technical or professional students can qualify after three years as skilled workers or mid-level technicians. Finishing this level qualifies them to enter technical colleges if they wish to improve their training. Students who choose to prepare for university enter a pre-university school, where they study for three years. All universities in Cuba are public, of the same status, and administered by the government. Universities offer bachelors, masters, and doctorate degrees.

Teachers must complete a five-year training course in either primary or secondary education. University professors must be experts in their fields, but they also receive teacher training and attend upgrading courses throughout their careers. This makes the quality of Cuban education, at all levels, one of the best in the hemisphere.

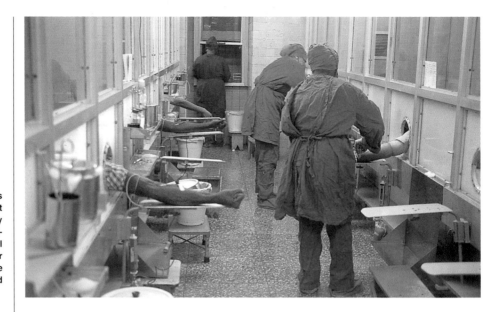

Cuban hospital workers take blood samples to test for the AIDS virus. They use Cuban-invented devices for tests—a small computer blood screener capable of detecting the presence of HIV in blood at an early stage.

HEALTH CARE

All Cubans are entitled to free comprehensive health care as part of the mandate of the revolution. Cuba's quality of health care is ranked among the best in the world and is unsurpassed in Latin America. Medical training is a popular course of study, and the education system has produced an abundance of physicians, both generalists and specialists.

Castro has twice been awarded the Health for All medal from the World Health Organization (WHO) and was the first head of state to receive one. He received the first medal in 1988 for achieving health standards in Cuba that WHO had set as goals for developing countries by the year 2000. Cuba met these targets in 1983, 17 years ahead of schedule. In 1998 Castro earned the second medal for having more Cuban doctors serving abroad than the WHO itself had and for reducing infant mortality considerably.

INTERNATIONAL COMMITMENT

Cubans are not the only ones to benefit from state-funded education, research, and medical care. Cuba is often the first country to respond to a medical crisis in the world, sending doctors, nurses, mobile hospitals, and vaccines whenever it can. Due to the U.S. embargo on trade in medicines to

Cuba, the country established its own biomedical research industry in the mid-1980s. This industry produced the first meningitis-B vaccine. Today it exports a low-cost hepatitis-B vaccine to over 30 countries and is developing anti-cancer therapies. With even tighter restrictions on imported medications today, Cuba has turned to expanding its knowledge and use of natural remedies. Pharmaceutical experts predict that the country is among the most likely sources of future breakthroughs in drug therapies.

Necessity rather than conservation very likely prompted this farmer to use a car tire for his waggon. In Cuba, savings are made by constantly recycling used items.

AIDS

When AIDS was first diagnosed on the island in 1985, the government treated it like any other unknown epidemic and isolated people in sanatoriums, where patients received medical care, shelter, and food. After learning more about transmission of the disease, AIDS patients were given the choice to live secluded or return to their communities. Since then Cuba has managed to instill a better understanding of the virus among Cubans, educate patients so that they act responsibly, and lessen the stigma attached to AIDS and its patients. Some patients have chosen to return to their families and their work or school lives, while others have chosen to stay in the sanatoriums because food is plentiful and the care is superior.

Cuba has one of the lowest AIDS transmission rates in the world, although it is surrounded by neighbors who are extensively affected by the virus. Cuban researchers have designed their own diagnosis procedure and are working hard on a vaccine.

RELIGION

FORMAL CHURCH RELIGION does not play an important role in the cultural life of Cuba. The Spanish brought Catholicism to the island, but today the majority of Cubans are atheists, believers of African religions, or non-practicing Catholics. Christmas interfered with the sugar harvest season, so it was officially abolished in 1969.

CATHOLIC CHURCH AND STATE

Article 8 of the Cuban constitution proclaims that "the State recognizes, respects, and guarantees religious freedom." The Cuban government does not, however, do anything to encourage the influence of the Catholic Church in Cuban life. Under the Spanish, the Church was part of the colonial establishment and consequently lost favor with many people. After the Spanish, but long before the revolution, there was growing disenchantment among Cubans about the way the Church failed to champion the needs of the poor who made up the majority of the population. Some priests did, however, speak out against the injustices under the Batista regime. In fact, a Catholic priest served as a chaplain with the revolutionaries in the Sierra Maestra. Catholics and priests also served as members in Castro's revolution.

As the country became more socialist, the Catholic Church became more hostile. In 1960 the rule of Castro was formally denounced in a pastoral letter that was read out at all services. Castro responded by declaring, "Whoever betrays a revolution such as ours betrays Christ and would be capable of crucifying him again."

Opposite: **A Cuban lady lights a candle at the Virgin of Charity of Cobre Church in Havana. The saint is also known as Oshun, the Santeria deity renowned for her sexual conquests.**

Below: **The Cuban flag is given a prominent place on the altar of a Roman Catholic church.**

In the 1960s the power of the Church was regulated by the new government. The number of priests was reduced by 70 percent, and church schools were replaced by government ones that excluded any religious education.

Many of the churches do not conduct religious services and function mainly as places of architectural interest. For a long time it was considered incompatible for a Cuban to hold allegiance to the Church and to the revolutionary State.

The peaceful grounds of Cathedral de la Sanctissima in Trinidad. Many churches open their doors for worship only on weekends.

RECENT CHANGES

In the 1990s the government relaxed its attitude toward the Church, perhaps because the Church has unbent a little from its anti-government position. The 1992 amendment to the constitution included a ban on religious discrimination and allowed practicing Catholics to become members of the Communist Party.

Since the collapse of the Soviet Union observers have noticed an increased interest in all forms of religion by Cubans. This may be related to the harsh economic climate.

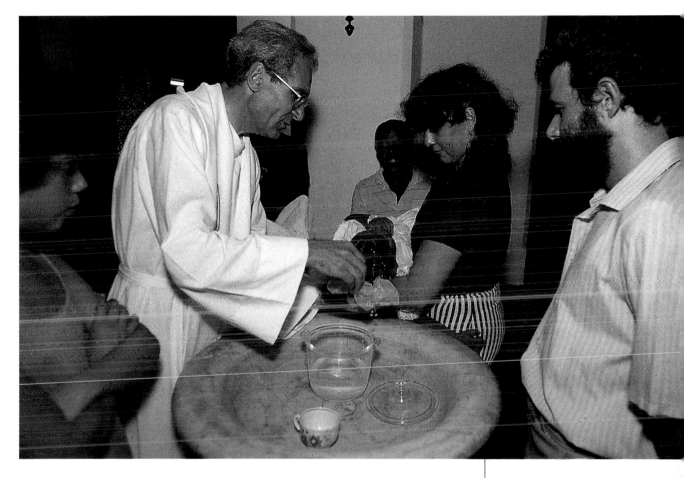

Upon Castro's invitation, Pope John Paul II visited Cuba for the first time in 1998. This was a signficant event for Cuban Catholics and raised hopes of better relations between the Church and the State. Christmas was restored as a national holiday the previous year in preparation for the papal visit, and Christmas celebrations have increased since then. The number of baptisms is increasing, and more Cubans are beginning to request church burials. An important expression of religious devotion is seen in the pilgrimages to St. Lazarus's sanctuary, just outside Havana.

In 1993 and 2003 the Church issued pastoral letters that spoke against the government. These letters elicited harsh criticism or some form of retaliation from the State. Church-State relations remain uncertain. Generally, however, the Catholic Church continues to keep a low profile.

A human skull and a bell are part of a voodoo ritual.

AFRO-CUBAN RELIGIONS

The thousands of slaves transported to Cuba by the Spanish brought their religions with them. The Catholic Church was tolerant toward these non-Christian beliefs, partly because the African religions were receptive to some aspects of Catholicism, and a synthesis of sorts took place.

Pedro Agustin Morell de Santa Cruz, a bishop of Cuba between 1753 and 1768, witnessed a rebellion of slaves and saw good reason for tolerating some aspects of African theology. If some tolerance were shown, he thought, there would be less resentment by the slaves and in time their beliefs would wither away. Under Morell, the Christian celebration of Epiphany (January 6) became a festival for slaves where they were allowed to elect symbolic chiefs and perform religious dances.

It is possible that church authorities were misled as to the extent and depth of this synthesis. Catholicism never took deep root among Cubans, while the African religions flourished and spread to non-black Cubans. Today forms of Afro-Cuban religions are commonly practiced by Cubans of all ethnic origins. There are no official figures, but as many as half to three-quarters of all Cubans subscribe to Afro-Cuban beliefs.

When white Cubans began to attend ceremonies in large numbers a catchphrase developed to explain their presence: *"Yo no creo pero lo repito"* (yoh noy KRAY-oh PAYR-roh loh ray-PEE-toh), or "I do not believe but I repeat the ritual."

THE VOODOO ELEMENT

Voodoo, the popular religion of neighboring Haiti, also has a presence in Cuba. Its influence can be traced back to the early 19th century, when whites fled from a black revolution in Haiti. Many fled as refugees to the eastern Oriente Province of Cuba, where they settled and continued to practice their belief in voodoo. At the beginning of the 20th century, the sugar industry in Cuba recruited hundreds of thousands of new black workers from Haiti, and voodoo in Cuba was given a fresh impetus.

Voodoo is a blending of Catholicism with traditional West African beliefs and involves the ritual invoking of the voodoo spirit world through magical prayers and rites. Devotees are believed to be capable of being possessed by spirits and sent into a trance. Believers sometimes place voodoo dolls by the side of trees in cemeteries. Their real significance is often disguised by the outward incorporation of Christian symbols, such as the sign of the cross, on the dolls.

SOME AFRO-CUBAN RELIGIONS Roman Catholicism is being increasingly challenged by Santería, an African religious cult that includes aspects of Catholicism, notably saint worship.

Two other African religions practiced in Cuba are Palo Monte and Abakua. Palo Monte, also known as the Mayombe cult, originates from the Bantu people of what is now Angola. Adherents of this secretive religion are referred to as *paleros* (pa-LAYR-rohs) or *congos* (KOHN-gos) and undergo an initiation ceremony. In common with contemporary beliefs of Bantu people in Africa, there is a strong reliance on the power of black magic, and this characterizes many of the rites.

A religion open to males only is Abakua. It originates from Nigeria and Benin in Africa, although at the present time the majority of its adherents in Cuba are white Cubans. Some observers play down the spiritual aspects of the religion, claiming that self-interest rather than theology binds the members together. It has been compared to the Mafia in terms of its influence and methods. An obligatory part of the initiation ceremony once involved the new member killing the first person he met.

There are no established places of worship for these religions, and while they are tolerated by the government, they do not receive any official support. Abakua, especially, is viewed with some suspicion as a potentially subversive group.

In the African Cuban cult of Santería, the Virgin Mary is an *orisha*, or saint, of the underworld.

SANTERÍA

The literal meaning of Santería is the way of the saints, and the religion is traced back to the Yoruban region of Nigeria in West Africa, the original home of the first slaves destined for Cuba. Over the centuries Santería has mixed its Yoruban spirit worship and magic practices with those from other parts of Africa, especially the Cameroons, and Cuba's neighbor Haiti. The most potent mix, however, has been with Spanish Catholicism.

The number of gods and goddesses worshiped stretches into the hundreds, but about a dozen have emerged as more important to contemporary Cubans. The primary ritual associated with Santería is a dance accompanied by drum music. Dance allows the participants to imitate and role-play events from traditional stories about the lives and deeds of the gods. Different types of drums have special qualities, often magical ones, and are associated with certain gods.

The traditional place of worship is the *cabildo* (ka-BEEL-doh), a cross between a church and a drinking club. While some aspects of Santería's devotional practices are remarkably Christian in character, others are recognizably African. It is not uncommon for mass hysteria to develop at large gatherings, and devotees, convinced of being possessed, may dress in the clothes associated with their god.

Orisha *with specific Christian counterparts include Oya—Saint Teresa, Osain—Saint Joseph, Orula—Saint Francis, Eleggua—Saint Anthony, Ogún—Saint John the Baptist, Shango—Saint Barbara, and Esu—Satan.*

ORISHA

Called *orisha* (hor-ISH-ah), the gods and goddesses are known also as saints. This is a result of the synthesis that occurred when the African beliefs absorbed some aspects of Catholic theology and practice. Christ became Olofi and the Virgin Mary was associated with Yemaya, goddess of the sea and mother of the *orisha* and the world. Acts of homage were made by slaughtering animals. Important deities were closely identified with certain colors. Ochun, or Oshun, was a beautiful goddess whose color was yellow. She was known for her sexual conquests and yet managed to merge with Caridad, the Christian patron saint of charity who is also renowned for her virginity, and who is also Cuba's patron saint.

People choose a particular *orisha* to worship and display their allegiance by wearing beads of the *orisha's* color around the neck or wrist. Like the Christian saints, each *orisha* has its own special date that functions as an anniversary. The anniversary calls for acts of adoration, and a devout believer keeps a shrine at home and decorates it colorfully on that day. Small symbolic offerings of food are laid at the foot of the shrine, candles are lit, and prayers are said.

Jugo natural 215 ML — 0,50

Dulce en almibar 4 onz. — 0,50

naranja pelada UNIDAD — 0,25

Petit Jamon ... 5,00 2 onz.

Petit D'Jamon ... 2,50

LANGUAGE

THE MOST OBVIOUS LEGACY OF CUBA'S colonial past is the Spanish language. First came the conquistadors, missionaries, and sailors; then the merchants and farmers. All spoke Spanish and permanently imposed their language on the island. A similar process occurred on other Caribbean islands and in most of Latin America.

Today Spanish is spoken by all Cubans and is also the language of government and commerce. English, Cuba's second language, is taught in all the schools and required for entrance to university.

Russian used to be taught in schools, but it was never very popular. Many Cubans learned Russian when they traveled to the Soviet Union to be trained as scientists and engineers.

The growing importance attached to tourism has increased the use and appeal of English among many Cubans. In this sense a cycle has been completed, for before the revolution, English was widely spoken for the same reason. Older Cubans who had been involved in the lucrative U.S. tourist trade are finding that their second language is once more in demand.

Opposite: **A restaurant displays its hanging menu in Spanish.**

Below: **Cuban boys take the opportunity to earn a little foreign exchange and brush up their language skills at the same time by helping tourists.**

SPANISH PRONUNCIATION

Pronouncing words in Spanish is easy because basically all the letters are pronounced, subject to some clear rules. The letter *h* is never pronounced, so the capital of Cuba is pronounced ah-BAN-ah. The letter *j* is pronounced as an aspirated (meaning, pronounced breathily) *h*, so the popular male name José is pronounced hoh-SAY.

The same rule applies to the letter *g* when it is followed by an *e* or *i*. For example, the word *gigante* (giant) is pronounced hee-GAN-tay. When speaking Spanish there is little difference between the letter *v* and the letter *b*, so the word *vino* (wine) is pronounced BEE-noh.

CORRECT STRESS Knowing where to place the stress in a word is governed by a systematic rule. Words ending in a vowel or *n* or *s*—the majority of words in Spanish—always receive a stress on the next to last syllable. For instance, the word for president, *presidente*, is pronounced pray-zee-DAYN-tay. All words that end in any consonant except *n* or *s* always receive the stress on the last syllable. If a word breaks this rule and is to be stressed on any other syllable, the change is signified by an accent over the vowel to be stressed. Guantánamo, for example, is pronounced gwan-TAN-a-moh, while Guantanamero (a citizen of Guantánamo) is pronounced gwan-ta-na-MAYR-roh.

One mark above a letter that affects pronunciation is the tilde. This is a small wave above the *n* that appears in words like España (Spain) and *mañana* (tomorrow). It changes the sound of the letter *n* to *ny*, so that the word for tomorrow is pronounced man-YA-na.

A news vendor on a Havana street with a pile of the leading newspaper *Granma* on his lap.

CUBAN SPANISH

The first Spaniards to settle in Cuba came from the southern part of Spain known as Andalusia. Although centuries have passed since they first arrived, they have left a deep influence on the way Cubans speak Spanish. A chief characteristic of Cuban Spanish is the relaxation of consonants, especially at the end of words, and the running together of words. While this is a general characteristic of Spanish in Latin America, it is particularly noticeable in Cuba. Visitors who speak European Spanish often find the pronunciation in Cuba more difficult to adjust to than in other Spanish-speaking countries in Latin America and the Caribbean.

In European Spanish the letters *ce*, *ci*, and *z* have a soft *th* sound. A word like *cerveza*, meaning beer, is pronounced thayr-VAY-tha as if the speaker has a slight lisp. Cubans tend to drop the *th* sound altogether and replace it with an *s* sound, sayr-VAY-sa.

A characteristic of Cuban Spanish is the tendency to drop the pronunciation of the *s* at the end of words. This is becoming increasingly common throughout Latin America. Linguists predict that it is only a matter of time before the final *s* sound is eliminated altogether. It is natural to wonder, then, how the plural is distinguished from the singular. In the case of a word like *la mamá* (mother) it is usually the context that makes it clear whether one mother or a group of mothers (*las mamás*) is being referred to. Both words are pronounced ma-MA.

Books in Spanish at a Cuban bookshop.

CUBAN TALK

English	Cuban Spanish	Pronunciation
Hello	*hola*	oh-la
Goodbye	*adios*	ad-ee-OHS, with the final *s* very slightly pronounced
Pleased to meet you	*mucho gusto*	MOO-choh GOO-stoh
I am hungry	*tengo hambre*	TAYN-goh AM-bray
I don't speak Spanish	*no hablo español*	noh AB-loh ay-span-YOHL
United States	*Estados Unidos*	ay-STAD-ohs oo-NEE-dohs, with the final *s* of both words very slightly pronounced

"I'm staying!" A street sign to instill patriotism in Cuban citizens.

FORMS OF ADDRESS

In Spain the terms *señor* (sayn-YOR) and *señora* (sayn-YOR-a) are the common forms of address corresponding to Mr. and Mrs. These terms are used in Cuba but are regarded as rather formal. People generally prefer to use the term *compañero* (kohm-pan-YAYR-roh) or *compañera* (kohm-pan-YAYR-ra), both of which mean comrade.

Cuban surnames consist of two words, but it is only the first surname that is usually used. For example, the name of the country's president is Fidel Castro Ruz, but to Cubans and the rest of the world, he is referred to as just Fidel Castro. The unused part of the surname, Ruz, is his mother's second name.

When women marry, their third name, that is, the second part of their surname, is replaced by *de* followed by the husband's second name. If Miss María Suárez Prieto married Mr. Pedro Raul Maurell, she becomes Señora (Mrs.) María Suárez de Raul. As the third name is reserved for strictly formal occasions, by both men and women, it is usually not obvious from a woman's name whether she is married. The surname of Señora María Suárez Raul's children would be Raul Suárez.

BODY LANGUAGE

Using body language as a form of expression is an integral part of the Cuban communicative process. It is often used in an almost intuitive manner. For example, when a Cuban wants to refer to Fidel Castro the gesture of rubbing an imaginary beard will sometimes be used instead of his name or title. No ridicule or contempt is implied by such a gesture.

POLITICAL LANGUAGE

Cuba is a highly politicized country, and this is reflected in the use of banners, posters, and slogans to communicate political ideas. Poster art is highly developed in Cuba, usually accompanied by words but equally capable of communicating successfully through visuals alone.

During the 1960s, particularly, the use of posters to communicate with citizens was an aspect of daily life. The images were mounted in special poster stands and periodically changed, in the way that advertising posters are changed in the United States and other countries. Posters that were regarded as particularly successful in communicating ideas about political and social issues were reproduced in books and presented on billboards. Giant billboards erected before 1959 to carry advertising campaigns now bear provocative images about international solidarity.

When Cuba faced the threat of imminent invasion by U.S.-backed counter-revolutionaries in the 1960s, the political motto *Patria o Muerte* (PA-tree-a oh moo-AYR-tay)—Country or Death—was frequently used to instill a sense of patriotism and solidarity. The threat of invasion has since diminished, but the economic crisis has caused the motto to evolve into *Socialismo o Muerte*—Socialism or Death. Only the shortage of electricity prevents the motto from being lit up in neon, in the style of its predecessor.

The most iconic poster that Cuba has produced is that of revolutionary rebel Che Guevara. Posters of Guevara are found everywhere in Cuba, and his images have been reproduced on various items, such as key chains, matchboxes, and coins.

Street names also bear testimony to political attitudes. In the first year of Castro's rule many changes were made to the names of main streets that dated from the colonial influence of Spain and the United States. This tradition has continued. In 1973, for instance, Avienda Carlos III—named after a Spanish king—became Avienda Salvador Allende to commemorate the socialist president of Chile, who was deposed shortly after his election.

In conversation, when a Cuban wants to emphasize a point, the palms of the hand are sometimes smacked together and accompanied by a call of entra *(AYN-tra). It is not an aggressive gesture and is only used in a positive manner. Hissing in order to attract attention is quite conventional and is not an expression of disapproval.*

The natural use of body language is also apparent in Cubans' frequent handshaking. In many Western countries the handshake is often a formal gesture of politeness, but Cubans will use it as a measure of their intimacy with the other person. If the relationship is a close one the handshake will often be correspondingly elaborate. Friends of both sexes also greet each other with a kiss on both cheeks.

ARTS

THE RICH AND CREATIVE SIDE OF CUBAN culture is most apparent in the arts. Cuban music is the most accessible form of art for non-Spanish speakers, and together with dance, it expresses an essential aspect of Cuban art. The visual arts are equally forthright and adventurous.

CUBAN MUSIC

A festive occasion in Cuba not accompanied by music would be unimaginable. Listening and dancing to music comes naturally, for Cubans possess a rich musical tradition. Cuban singers and bands have a strong following in Latin America, and many of Cuba's top musicians regularly tour foreign countries. Professional musicians are employed by the State, and highly talented individuals receive the highest salaries.

The unique sound of Cuban music harks back to the music's origins in the Yoruban and Congolese cultures of West Africa, the original home of the Cuban slaves. It accounts for the distinctive use of percussion instruments and for the strong link between music and dance and the practices and beliefs of Santería.

Cuban bands usually have at least one guitar player, and this points to the other major influence on Cuba's music. The Spanish introduced the guitar, and with the instrument came the dramatic, vigorous Spanish flamenco sounds. Spanish influence also accounts for ballad singing.

Opposite. **Brightly colored figurines, trinkets, and paintings are on sale in a Havana craft market.**

Below: **Ballad singers serenade customers in restaurants in Havana. Ballads are also popular in the countryside.**

95

THE MUSIC OF *SON* *Son* (SOHN), the indigenous dance music of Cuba, goes back at least two centuries to its home in eastern Cuba. The soul of *son* music is African, but the Hispanic musical tradition has contributed to its evolution. The three distinguishing characteristics of *son* music are the rhythm tapped out on two heavy wooden sticks called claves, the solo vocal element requiring improvisation by the singer, and a repeated chorus toward the middle or end of the musical piece.

The wide range of musical instruments accommodated within *son* include the organ, accordion, flute, violin, trombone, and even the synthesizer. One of the lesser-known instruments used is the *tres* (TRAYS), a small three-string guitar. The *tres* produces a delicate, metallic timbre, one of the most recognizable sounds of *son*.

Son became internationally famous with the recording of *The Buena Vista Social Club*, produced by Ry Cooder, in 1997. This album features some of Cuba's best *son* singers, such as Compay Segundo.

Son-changüi (SOHN-chan-GWEE) was one of the earliest forms of *son* music that originally combined the *tres*, bongo, and maracas. Through the 20th century, other instruments, such as the trombone, were added to it. Elio Reve was a *son-changüi* musician who, in the late 1960s, was inspired to combine his music with *son-charanga* (SOHN cha-RANG-a) forms and instruments. *Son-charanga* is an early 20th-century form of *son* that adopted European influences and such instruments as the violin, woodwinds, and flute. *Son-charanga* combines a strong African- and Spanish-influenced rhythm with flute, violin, and piano improvisations. Elio Reve joined forces with Juan Formell in 1969 to form Los Van Van and create a new sound called *songo* (sohn-goh). *Songo* combines trombones, violins, and Cuban percussion with American funk, rock, and jazz sounds to create a vibrant popular sound in the contemporary Caribbean.

ALL THAT CUBAN JAZZ Cuban rhythms have influenced jazz since its birth, and from the 1930s the effect was especially decisive. The Dizzy Gillespie orchestra's popularity was enhanced by the incorporation of Cuban sounds in 1946. A few years later Stan Kenton, a prominent jazz musician, hired drummers from an Afro-Cuban band to make a hit record, *The Peanut Vendor*. After World War II New York and Cuban jazz deeply influenced each other. Today Cuban jazz takes many forms that depend on the major rhythm adopted. Famous names include Chucho Valdés, his group Irakere, and acclaimed pianist Gonzalo Rubalcava.

Los Van Van, a popular band in Cuba.

SALSA

Salsa music is derived from *son* and was brought by self-exiled Cubans to the United States, where it is currently enjoying a revival. It is far less pure than *son*, having absorbed extraneous rhythms such as soul and rock, and salsa fans are not conscious of its Cuban origin. Cubans discuss music in terms of how *sabroso* (sa-BROH-soh), or tasty, it is. This may explain the word salsa (sauce). The characteristic sound is a combination of fast piano pieces and multiple percussion instruments. If the band is a big one, guitars, horn, and double bass are added. The result is a small orchestra resembling the big bands that dominated the 1950s cabaret scene in Havana. Those who first exported salsa include members of such orchestras.

DANCE

Dance is as integral to Cuban culture as music is, and dancing the night away often literally describes what happens when Cubans are out to enjoy themselves. As with music, the origins of Cuban dance lie in both Africa and Spain. In Catholic-run colonies drum music and dancing by slaves were not regarded as morally unhealthy or politically dangerous as was sometimes true in the Protestant areas of the southern United States. Consequently, the intricate rhythms accompanying religious rituals were better preserved.

The link between music, dance, and religion is especially preserved in rumba, a form of music that originated among the communities of poor blacks in Havana around the turn of the century. It has been called the purest form of African music to have survived in Cuba.

Traditional rumba music takes different forms. The *yambú* (yam-BOO) is a relatively slow dance performed by two dancers. The *columbia* (koh-loom-BEE-a) is usually a men's dance and sometimes involves the use of machetes and knives. It is faster and more exciting than *yambú* and originates from the Matanzas region. The country's most famous rumba group is known as Los Muñequitos de Matanzas.

Other forms of popular dancing in Cuba can be traced back to Spain and France. The traditional French country dance known as *contradanza* (kohn-tra-DAN-sa) was introduced from Haiti. A slower Cuban version, equally classical and formal, is called *danzon* (dan-SOHN) and is related to the cha-cha. Dance forms like the cha-cha, conga, mambo, and tango are performed with artistic verve in Cuba.

BALLET   Ballet is also highly regarded in Cuba. The National Ballet Company ranks as one of the world's most talented dance companies and once had close links with the Bolshoi and Kirov ballet companies of Russia. The most prominent ballet personality in Central America is Alicia Alonso, a Cuban. She studied in Cuba and New York, where she made her professional debut. She was financially unsuccessful in running her own ballet company in Havana in the 1940s and left once again to work in New York. After the 1959 revolution she returned to Cuba and directed the National Ballet Company, which was given government subsidies.

Two other dance companies in Cuba are Camagüey Ballet and Cuban National Dance.

A tableau from the opera *The Merry Widow*, performed in Havana.

A Cuban political poster from the 1960s supporting the Vietnam revolution displays the graphic revolutionary tradition of poster design.

POSTER ART

The pluralism of Cuban art is best represented in the visual arts. The posters and paintings of native and self-exiled artists demonstrate a unique combination of Afro-American, Indo-American, and Euro-American traditions. During the 1980s there were exciting developments as artists expressed new themes and questioned the centralized state bureaucracy. The current climate of economic hardship has not inspired dramatic artistic achievements.

The period between 1965 and 1975 has been called the golden age of the poster. Artists still express themselves in this medium, as the tradition is an ongoing one, but in the past Cuban posters had a dramatic international impact. This was partly due to the content, which focused on the achievements of the 1959 revolution and stressed national liberation movements around the world. Equally impressive was the embracing of avant-garde traditions like pop art, minimalism, and surrealism. The rigid dogma that was stifling art in the Soviet Union, by imposing simplistic techniques and themes, was publicly rejected in Cuba by Che Guevara, the revolutionary leader from Argentina who worked closely with Castro. Some of the most celebrated of all Cuban posters are those depicting Guevara.

Surrealism, a European art movement characterized by dream-like images that often appear to explore the unconscious mind, has influenced Cuban painters. A similar kind of movement in literature, known as magic realism, has been very influential among Latin American writers and has also affected the form of art in Cuba. A good example is a poster for a movie, *The Death of a Bureaucrat*, painted by Alfredo Rostgaard. In the picture the bureaucrat's head is replaced by a hand that points up to a gravestone. The poster and the movie satirize bureaucracy and suggest the need for a breakup of centralized power.

PAINTING

One of Cuba's most famous artists is Wilfredo Lam, who was part of the post-World War II surrealist movement. One of his works, *La Jungle*, is in the Museum of Modern Art in New York. In paintings, he set out, in his own words, "to paint the drama of my country, but by thoroughly expressing the Negro spirit, the beauty of the plastic art of the blacks." Lam died in 1982, but a contemporary artist, Manuel Mendive, is consciously building on a similar Afro-Cuban aesthetic. His 1982 work, *Untitled*, is an example of his weaving together of African and Cuban themes.

Raúl Martínez is the painter who introduced pop art into Cuba. In *The Island*, painted in 1970, he presents a group portrait of anonymous Cuban citizens alongside such prominent individuals as Castro, Che Guevara, and the North Vietnamese leader Ho Chi Minh. Its political message is that all Cuban people are equally important, and no one person should have a special heroic status. Martínez also paints posters, and one of his most famous calls for the end of machismo.

Many Cuban artists work abroad, especially in neighboring countries, such as Mexico. Most of them are not political exiles, and many return regularly to Cuba. An example is José Bedia, who explains, "If I am living here during the 'special [austerity] period' I should spend my time looking for food, not paint and canvas."

When modernist art was being denounced by Eastern European and Soviet leaders, Fidel Castro declared, "Our enemies are capitalists and imperialists, not abstract art."

LITERATURE

Several generations of Cubans grew up studying European and American literature but were not exposed to their native literary traditions. Cuban literature existed, but not many educated Cubans appreciated it.

After 1959, when the revolutionary government took over, Cubans were encouraged to read books with themes of revolution or equality. Students of Cuban literature are encouraged to read Cirilo Villaverde's *Cecilia Valdés*, a novel about an ill-fated romance between a mulatto woman and a Spanish-Cuban aristocrat.

Contemporary writers, like all other artists in Cuba, work independently but are salaried by the state. The shortage of paper after the Soviet collapse had severely curtailed publication, but previously a successful novel sold 40,000 to 80,000 copies. This is extraordinarily high for a country with a population of only 11.3 million.

POETRY

Poetry's wide appeal is shown by the regular publication of poems in newspapers and magazines. The nationalist hero of the 19th century, José Martí, is also a revered poet. Children are first introduced to his romantic lyric poems in school. A respect for poetry is an accomplishment that most Cubans maintain throughout adult life.

> With the poor of the earth
> I am happy with my lot:
> The mountain stream
> Pleases me more than the sea.
> —José Martí, *The Temple of the Mountain*

Nicolás Guillén, a mulatto born in 1902, was one of the Caribbean's best-known poets. He was Cuba's poet laureate until his death in 1989. Other poets, such as Nancy Morejón, have achieved recognition. Morejón combines romantic themes with revolutionary commitment and echoes the work of José Martí.

A number of literary competitions are held annually, and winning writers are guaranteed the publication of their book. A highly literate population in a remarkably politicized country provides a very sophisticated readership. It also promotes a healthy literary climate that nurtures new writers and sustains established ones.

Important writers include the novelist Alejo Carpentier (1906–80) and the poet José Lezama Lima (1910–76). The novels of Carpentier, a former journalist and diplomat, belong to an era of political ferment and have wide international appeal. They include *Kingdom of the World*, *Explosion in a Cathedral*, and *Reasons of State*. Lima's poetry is more concerned with a search for the roots of Cuban identity. His most important work, *Paradiso*, has been translated into English.

Political thrillers are very popular with Cubans. In 1974, when two writers wrote the mystery thriller *The Fourth Circle*, the first print-run of 80,000 copies sold out within one month. One of the writers, Luis Rogelio Nogueras, later wrote a novel, *If I Die Tomorrow*, that had a plot involving a Cuban secret service agent infiltrating a group of anti-Castro terrorists.

"Unfortunately, reading is becoming an increasing luxury for the Cuban people themselves ... the country's lack of hard currency made it very difficult to purchase books from other countries. ... Cuban bookshops are closing, converting to other uses or putting up the prices of their dwindling stocks. ..."

—John Pateman, in a letter to The Bookseller *magazine, describing a "Books for Cuba Fund" launched in the United Kingdom for Cuban readers*

FILM CULTURE

The media in Cuba are controlled by the government. The informative quality of some newsreels and documentaries has been compromised by a desire to express only what is considered politically correct.

One of the major artistic developments since 1959 has been the successful creation of a thriving film culture. The government set up the Cuban Institute of Film Art and Industry, which was largely responsible for starting this development.

In the 1960s and 1970s full-length movies often had considerable artistic merit, as well as being free of ideological control by the government. Several Cuban films have received acclaim at international festivals, including *Memories of Underdevelopment* by Tomás Gutiérez Alea and *Lucia* by Humberto Solás, both of which were produced in 1968.

Strawberry and Chocolate, by Alea and Juan Carlos Tabio, won the Special Jury Prize at the 1994 Berlin International Film Festival. Juan Carlos Cremata's *Nothing* received recognition at the 2003 Miami International Film Festival when it received the jury's Grand Award.

ART FESTIVALS

Every other December Havana dances to the sounds of the International Jazz Festival. Aficionados of jazz from all over the world descend on the city and join over a thousand Cuban fans for a festival of listening, dancing, and drinking rum. Jazz festivals are held all over the world, but the annual event in Havana inspires particular respect among devotees of this type of music.

Non-jazz music festivals are held annually at the tourist resort town of Varadero on the north coast. These include the Varadero International Music Festival and Electroacoustic Music Festival.

The Habana Bienal (Havana Biennial) is an important international arts festival that features exhibitions of paintings, other art forms, and conferences, and is an expression of Cuba's commitment and support to

Third World cultural development. Latin American artists provide two-thirds of the total work shown.

Cuba also sponsors the annual International Festival of the New Latin American Cinema. It is a prestigious event that brings together filmmakers and critics from all over the world. People come not only to view new films but also to attend conferences and critical debates on film theory and practice. Hollywood figures occasionally attend, and past guests have included Francis Ford Coppola. The festival usually opens in the old-style Hotel Nacional in Havana with Castro in attendance.

Equally prestigious, but in the field of ballet, is the annual Havana International Ballet Festival. It was started in 1960 and continues to attract major ballet companies from all around the world.

Mural adaptation of Raúl Martínez's *The Island* outside a Havana exhibition center.

LEISURE

LIKE PEOPLE ALL OVER THE WORLD, Cubans find a variety of ways to enjoy themselves when not at work. Athletic games are popular with all sections of society, and the government actively promotes sports at all levels. More relaxing pursuits include dancing and listening to music. At home, Cubans enjoy the company of friends and neighbors, and leisure time is regarded as well-spent if animated by good conversation.

BASEBALL

Baseball is Cuba's most popular sport. The game was introduced to the island from the United States in the 19th century, although evidence suggests that Indian tribes like the Cuban Taínos played a ball game similar to baseball. The game of batey was played by the Taínos on a stone-lined paved court.

Before 1959 the best teams in Cuba were linked to U.S. leagues. Scouts of top U.S. teams regularly searched Cuba for young players to sign. Many turned out to be highly talented players who later made successful careers with major league teams.

A Cuban pitcher for the Cincinnati Reds, Dolf Luque, was with the team for more than a decade. He was the first Cuban-born player to play in the major leagues. Other famous Cuban players of the period leading up to the revolution include Minnie Minoso of the Chicago White Sox and Camilo Pascual of the Washington Senators.

Despite the severing of relations with the United States there has been no drop in Cuban enthusiasm for baseball. It remains the national sport, and every large town has a stadium that fills up for baseball games. The rules are exactly the same as those in the United States, but there are some surprising differences. No fee is charged for admission to a game and fans are likely to cheer teams with cries of *Socialismo o Muerte*!

"Sports are an antidote to vice."
—*Fidel Castro*

Opposite: **Cuban boys have fun fishing and swimming.**

107

Cuba's national team is always a contender for a medal at the Olympic Games. Indeed, the Cuban National Team has become the team to watch in recent years, taking home gold medals in 1992, 1996, and 2004. They lost to the United States in 2000. Cuban players can also be found on professional teams in the United States, where high salaries are a definite attraction.

Weekends are the time to play with young and old. Amateur and professional players turn out to fill the many baseball parks and stadiums around the country. Every school competes in interschool leagues, and local community groups organize their own competitions.

Cuba encourages sports by providing facilities, such as basketball courts.

PLAYING THE GAME

Cubans engage in many other games besides baseball in their leisure time. Basketball comes a close second in popularity. The 17th Caribbean Basketball Championships were held in Cuba for the first time in 2004. Both the Cuban men's and women's teams emerged as the winners.

A tradition of playing chess is still upheld in Cuba. A youngster may first learn the game in junior high school, and public chess tables in parks are often used for games between senior citizens.

Soccer has not caught the imagination of young Cubans, but is actively encouraged by the government. The game is so identified with Latin America that Cuba's relative lack of interest in the game seems an anomaly.

Tennis, squash, wrestling, fencing, swimming, rowing, and volleyball are some other popular sports usually first encountered in school. Wrestling and fencing are particularly popular, and on weekends there is usually a match in a town gymnasium. Even a small town has at least one gymnasium. Often a temporary ring is set up in a town square to host a local tournament. Horseracing is also popular, but since gambling was outlawed in 1959, few engage in it.

A three-walled court game enjoyed immensely by players and spectators alike is jai alai, which came to Cuba from the Basque region of Spain. It is a very fast game, for two or more players, that depends on quick reflexes and speed. Using a 2-foot (0.6 m) wicker basket strapped to the hand, players try to hit a small hard ball against the front wall of the court so that their opponents are unable to return it and thus lose a point.

Track and field, along with baseball and boxing, has made Cuba internationally famous. National teams regularly take first place in the Central American and Caribbean Games, and are often the favorites to win events at the Pan American Games. The highlight of Cuba's international presence in sports came in 1991 when it hosted the Pan American Games. National teams from North America and South America, including the United States, participated. Cuba can also be guaranteed to return from the Olympics with a cluster of gold, silver, and bronze medals. The best sporting year for Cuba was in 1992 at the Barcelona Olympics, when it won 31 medals, 14 of which were gold. Cuba received nine gold medals out of a total of 27 at the Athens Olympics in 2004. Between 1900 and 2004, Cuba has garnered a total of 170 medals in Olympic competitions.

Chess enjoyed a high status in Cuba during the 30 years of close economic and cultural cooperation with the Soviet Union.

THE ART OF RELAXING

The art of relaxing is an attractive aspect of Cuban culture that finds expression in a variety of ways. A rocking chair is a common item on the verandah or balcony of a Cuban home. People like to sit in the comfort of their homes and pass the time of day with like-minded neighbors or family acquaintances. Friendship and friendly conversation are highly regarded in life.

Even more emblematic of contentment is the picture of a relaxed individual seated in a comfortable rocking chair and smoking a Cuban

BOXING

This pugilistic tradition existed in Cuba before 1959, when it was mainly the sport of middle- and upper-class men. After the revolution, when the sport was nurtured by the state and made available to all classes, its popularity increased.

Over the years Cuba has produced some outstanding boxers, including featherweight Kid Chocolate (Eligio Sardinias Montalbo) and welterweights Kid Gavilan (Walter Gerardo Gonzalez), Benny Paret, and Luis Rodriguez. The most successful was Teofilo Stevenson, who was three times Olympic heavyweight champion—in 1972, 1976, and 1980.

As in other sports in Cuba, there is no clear-cut distinction between amateur and professional players. There are no professional athletes, however, the government attaches a lot of importance to sports, both as a form of fitness and leisure as well as a source of national pride and achievement. Talented individuals are encouraged to devote themselves full-time to a particular sport. During this time they receive a salary and in many respects function as professionals. After his initial success, this was the case with Stevenson.

Boxing is first introduced to young boys at school. Those who show skill and interest are usually encouraged to train by preparing for a local tournament. The country's major boxing competition is the Giraldo Cordova Cardin Tournament, and leading boxers are expected to prove themselves at this annual event.

cigar. The enjoyment of a fine cigar is regarded by tobacco users as deeply satisfying, and Cubans are blessed—as well as cursed, in terms of the damage to their health—by ready access to the best cigars in the world. Castro was a dedicated smoker for many years; he was invariably featured holding a huge cigar in his hand or mouth. In his own words, "after a truly heroic struggle," he managed to quit the habit, but for many Cubans leisure time without a cigar is unthinkable.

The most popular type of cigar is known as a torpedo—about half an inch (1.2 cm) thick, four inches (10 cm) long, and closed at both ends—and is very cheap. Cigars are smoked mainly by men and can last for an hour or more. Cuban cigars, especially the better quality ones that sell for $20 each, used to be very popular in the United States but can no longer be sold there.

CUBAN CIGARS

The Taino Indians smoked tobacco and passed the habit on to the Spanish settlers, who in turn introduced the idea to Europe. As smoking became increasingly popular and fashionable, the foundations for Cuba's cigar industry were laid. The reputation for excellence associated with Cuban and especially Havana cigars is unrivaled anywhere in the world. Famous personalities, such as American writer Ernest Hemingway, who lived for years in Cuba, extolled their virtues. Other famous Cuban cigar addicts include American comedian Groucho Marx and British prime minister Winston Churchill.

The majority of cigars are machine-produced, but rolling a cigar by hand is still a highly regarded skill. All cigars bear a colored ring that denotes their quality. Cuban men choose a cigar because of its strength and flavor. The word *oscuro* (os-KUR-o) means dark, but when applied to cigars it means black and very strong; *maduro* (mad-UR-o) means ripe, and this describes a brown-black cigar with full-bodied flavor; *colorado* (kolo-RAD-o) means red, and is a reddish-brown, aromatic cigar; *claro* (KLAR-o) means clear, and denotes a mild-flavored cigar.

Cigar aficionados also claim that the size and shape of a Cuban cigar affect its flavor. Apart from the very popular torpedo, named after its shape, there is the corona cigar with straight sides and one end closed. The perfecto is cylindrical and tapered, with a half-pointed head.

Cigar factories have a tradition of entertaining and educating cigar makers as they work by having readers recite passages from books. Another tradition is that employees smoke freely as they work and take home a couple of cigars each day. The average life expectancy in Cuba is 77, but it is a lot shorter for cigar makers. Cuba sets high quality standards for its cigars, and this limits the number of cigars it produces.

A NIGHT OUT

A Casa de la Trova is a cross between a bar, a dance hall, and a small concert hall. These centers are open from around 9 P.M. to midnight. They are very popular on weekends, when they also are open during lunchtime. Most large towns and cities have a Casa de la Trova.

A trova is a classical ballad. In times gone by, troubadours traveled from town to town to recite their ballads to the accompaniment of music. Traditional troubadours are still to be found, but today the range of songs and music is far wider. The *nueva trova* (new-ABE-a TRO-ba) has introduced post-revolution themes into the songs, and there is a blues version of the *trova* known as *filin* (FIL-in). Distinguished Cuban troubadours include Faustino Oramas and Pedro Luis Ferrer.

A lot of entertainment available to Cubans in their leisure time is free of charge. There is no admission fee to attend a sports event or enter a Casa de la Trova. Places that do charge admission, such as the cinema and theater, are not run as profit-making businesses. The cost of a ticket to see a film or a play is a far smaller proportion of a person's income than it is in the United States or Europe. As a consequence, cultural establishments like theaters are patronized by a wide cross-section of the population.

Perhaps for this reason, the distinction between highbrow and popular culture does not apply in Cuba. Places of entertainment that are often associated with particular income levels in other countries are frequented by Cubans of all classes.

Young Cubans get into the swing of things at a dance.

FESTIVALS

FEW ASPECTS OF LIFE REMAINED THE SAME after the flight of Batista on January 1, 1959. The government headed by Fidel Castro abolished many of the public holidays and replaced them with new ones that commemorated important events in the country's history.

The most dramatic consequence of these changes was the demise of religious festivals that had once played an important role in the social life of Cubans. Christmas Day, for instance, was not celebrated for many years. It returned to the calendar only in 1997 to prepare for the visit of Pope John Paul II the following year.

The desire to celebrate did not disappear but was channelled into the new holidays that marked achievements important to all Cubans. Living with economic uncertainties means people cannot spend as much money as they used to, but the spirit of enjoyment remains undiminished.

Above: **Children at an art competition. Such events are held on anniversary holidays, and everyone can participate.**

Opposite: **Cuban women dress up in colorful traditional costumes and accessories.**

REMEMBRANCE OF THE NATIONAL REVOLUTION

Havana and Santiago de Cuba mount the most colorful celebrations for Cuba's major annual festival on July 26. Cubans pour into these cities from the countryside to join in the festivities. For weeks before, people are busy preparing fantastic costumes and making the floats that are a highlight of the parades. Across the island, groups of people based around a place of work, an organization, or a residential district strive to produce the most flamboyant and eye-catching displays. A sense of pride accompanies these efforts, and tremendous enthusiasm is generated.

HISTORY OF A HOLIDAY

Cuba's most important holiday lasts from July 25 to July 27. Known as Remembrance of the National Revolution, this period celebrates an event that took place six years before the actual overthrow of Batista. On July 26, 1953, a group of about 150 revolutionaries led by Fidel Castro launched an attack on the Moncada Barracks just outside the city of Santiago de Cuba. Militarily, the attack was a dismal failure. The rebels had neither the experience nor the weapons to successfully capture the army post, and many of them were shot and killed by Batista's army. Others were captured and tortured to death. Castro escaped but was captured a week later and imprisoned. Ironically, the failed attack was to prove successful in its ultimate aim of igniting a revolutionary spirit among Cuban people. Black and red flags began to appear marked M•26•7, indicating the birth of the Movement of July 26, and the struggle against Batista was resumed with renewed determination.

July 26, along with the day before and after, is a national celebration across Cuba. Posters and flags appear long before the day, still bearing the legend M•26•7, and festival events are organized in every community. What helps to make the event so spectacular an occasion is that this part of the year had been a festive occasion long before the attack on the Moncada Barracks. Previously, it marked the time of the important sugar festival and was traditionally a time for relaxation and celebration. This was why the rebels chose July 26 for their attack; they hoped to catch the soldiers unprepared and too drunk to fight back.

Dances form an essential part of the celebrations. While some dance troupes are professional, the majority are formed by local groups that practice and rehearse with amateur musicians. Dance and music are integral parts of Cuban culture enjoyed by young and old. Even when economic conditions are bad, Cubans come out on July 26 to sing and dance and enjoy themselves. Traditionally, an abundance of food accompanies street parties. Vendors set up stalls selling barbecued pork, a Cuban party favorite, barbecued goat, and whistles and party favors for children. Along with a plentiful supply of rum and beer, these mark the occasion as a special celebration.

CARNIVAL

The July 26 Remembrance of the National Revolution holiday coincides with a traditional carnival that goes back a long way in Cuban history, as far back as 1493, when Christopher Columbus visited Cuba a second time, bringing sugarcane from the Canary Islands.

Before the advent of machine harvesting, all the sugarcane had to be cut by hand using wide-bladed machetes. It was a back-breaking and exhausting occupation. Once the cane was cut, the workers could enjoy a period of rest, and because this was the time they received their wages, it was natural to celebrate.

The workers on the sugar plantations were originally all slaves from Africa, and the dances and music of Carnival can be traced back to traditional tribal festivities from West Africa. Havana and Santiago de Cuba are the most important places where these traditional celebrations are actively preserved. In Santiago de Cuba there is even a museum devoted to preserving memories and artifacts connected to the songs and dances of the July carnival. The drum is especially prominent in Carnival celebrations in Cuba.

During the crisis in the early 1990s, Carnival festivities had to be limited. As Cuba found ways to get by without Soviet support and increased its domestic food production, these celebrations have returned to the island with a good part of their former pomp and grandeur.

Cubans—some in Castro beards, and at least one wearing the M.26.7 armband—salute their leader at an anniversary march.

Obviously enjoying their break from the school routine, these young Cubans are organized into flag-waving contingents for the celebration of political anniversaries.

PUBLIC HOLIDAYS

July 25 to 27 is by no means the only time when Cubans celebrate. There are four other official holidays, all of which have a political significance. These days are marked by a mixture of public speeches and partying.

Political leaders, including Fidel Castro and his brother Raúl, deliver keynote speeches to vast crowds of supporters. Such speeches are usually held in large open spaces, such as the Plaza de la Revolución in Santiago de Cuba. The atmosphere at these gatherings is genuinely festive. Both before and after the speeches the crowds are entertained with songs, dance, and music.

CALENDAR OF HOLIDAYS

1 January	Liberation Day (success of 1959 revolution)
1 May	Labor Day
25–27 July	Remembrance of the National Revolution
10 October	Day of Cuban Culture
25 December	Christmas Day was abolished in 1969 but was restored as a public holiday in 1997, one year before Pope John Paul II's visit.

COMPARSA

A *comparsa* (kohm-PAR-sa) is a theatrical term that covers the dance and music, as well as the performers, associated with a carnival. Traditionally, members of a community got together and organized a *comparsa* as their contribution to the local carnival. After weeks of rehearsals, the *comparsa* was ready for the public and took its part in the grand parade that wove its way through the town center.

While large-scale carnivals are no longer a regular feature of Cuban life, *comparsa* still contribute to special events on public holidays. Participants still adhere to the tradition of careful rehearsals to ensure a perfect performace on the actual day.

A sense of pride and a competitive spirit often accompany a *comparsa*. This goes back to the days when every big carnival included a competition for the best *comparsa*, judged by a local committee. The winning *comparsa* was usually the one displaying the most imaginative combination of costumes and dance.

The celebrations are extended to evening time, when parties are organized both inside and outside people's homes. There is usually a lot to eat and drink at these parties to contribute to the merry atmosphere.

Public holidays are also occasions for families to come together. January 1 is the most important day of the year in this respect. The first day of the year happens to coincide with the date of dictator Fulgencio Batista's departure from Cuba in 1959, and so it functions as an anniversary of the birth of the new regime.

Fidel Castro's speech is an essential part of the Remembrance of the National Revolution celebrations.

Notwithstanding its political significance, New Year's Day has always been a special day in Cuba. The last day of the year, December 31, is not an official holiday, but it tends to resemble one because so many people take the day off work to prepare for parties that night.

REINICIO DE LA GUERRA DE INDEPENDENCIA
·24 DE FEBRERO

PARA
LA PATRIA
NOS LEVANTAMOS

"For our country we will rise!" declares this sign commemorating the February 24 uprising of 1895.

FEBRUARY 24

Another important political anniversary is commemorated every February. Large posters remind Cubans of the anniversary of the Second War for Independence.

Plans for the February 24 rebellion were laid as early as January 5, 1892, when José Martí established the Cuban Revolutionary Party in New York, where he lived in exile. He and other exiled rebel leaders held several meetings in Jamaica and Costa Rica, and completed their plans on Christmas Day 1894. On February 24, 1895, uprisings began all over Cuba. The war lasted a few years. It cost the lives of Cuba's most colorful revolutionaries, but it achieved freedom for Cubans with the creation of the Republic of Cuba on May 20, 1902.

RELIGIOUS DAYS

Traditional religious festivals have either been completely abandoned or absorbed into days of secular celebration. January 6 used to be the celebration of the Feast of Kings, commemorating the day when the Three Kings brought gifts to the baby Jesus. Parents used to buy small surprise gifts for their children and presented them on the morning of January 6. Although the day now only has special significance for the small minority of Christians in the country, the tradition of exchanging gifts has not completely died out. However, it is more common for gifts to be given and received on July 26.

Before 1959 the most important religious festival was Holy Week, the week before Easter. In 1965 Holy Week was changed to Playa Giron Week and became the focus for periods of mass voluntary labor. Playa Giron is a small village very close to the site of the abortive Bay of Pigs invasion, which took place over the Easter period in 1961. In 1969 the Easter period became the Playa Giron Month, part of a campaign to increase the country's production of sugar. Currently it is known as the Playa Giron *Quince* (KEEN-say), meaning 15, to signify a two-week period of communal effort.

Christmas decorations adorn the facade of a church and draw attention to the crèche.

FOOD

IN COMMON WITH other aspects of the country's culture, the food of Cuba reveals the dual influence of Spain and Africa. From these two different culinary traditions, combined with locally available ingredients, a distinctive food style has emerged. Since the Special Period began in 1991, Cubans have struggled to produce enough to eat, and although they now get enough calories, some foods, such as milk, meat, and eggs, are still in short supply or are expensive.

CUBAN TASTES

Cuban tastebuds are not as attuned to hot food as neighboring Latin American countries. There is a partiality for spicy tastes, but compared to nearby Mexico, the result seems mild. Nevertheless, a pork chop, for instance, would never be prepared without a mixture of different spices being fried at the same time. Beans of various sorts are a regular favorite. *Congri* (KOHN-gree) is made from kidney beans, but black and white beans are also used.

Before the food shortages made any sort of meat expensive, a favorite meat was chicken. Crocodile meat is sometimes eaten, and the taste, somewhere between that of chicken and pork, is not exotic. Turtle meat is used to prepare stews and soups. Pizza is very popular as a quick lunchtime meal.

RICE WITH EVERYTHING

The most basic Cuban food item is rice. It forms the staple of most meals and is commonly served with beans. *Moros y cristianos* (MOHR-rohs ee kree-stee-AN-ohs)—Spanish for Moors and Christians—is the name given for a popular dish of white rice and black beans cooked together. The dish is named Moors and Christians because the ingredients are black and white. In this case the term Moor is used to mean a dark-skinned individual. Another rice dish that is as popular in modern Spain as it is in Cuba is *arroz con pollo* (a-ROHS kohn POHL-yoh), chicken with rice.

Picadillo (pee-ka-DEEL-yoh), Spanish for minced meat, uses ground beef mixed with green peppers, onions, tomatoes, and olives. Raisins are often mixed in with the rice, and sometimes a fried egg is laid over the rice.

A typical Cuban dinner table usually holds a white mound of rice.

124

THE FOOD REVOLUTION

The question of food security, or producing enough food to feed the population, has been problematic for much of Cuba's contemporary history. Since Cuba could not sell sugar to the United States after 1959, Cuba relied on a special relationship with the Soviet Union, in which the Soviets paid a premium for Cuban sugar (as much as five times the going world price) and allowed Cuba to buy unrefined petroleum in return. Cuba refined Soviet oil, used some locally, and exported the remainder. The export earnings were used to buy food. The sugar price was very attractive, so Cuba devoted the majority of its productive farmland to sugarcane and imported vast quantities of food. Half of Cuba's food supply was imported.

When this special deal ended with the Soviet collapse, Cuba faced serious food shortages that resulted in undernourishment. Beginning in 1991 with the Special Period, Cubans entered a vast national experiment to increase food production for domestic consumption. By 1995 the worst of the food crisis was over. One of the most dramatic changes to take place at this time was the creation of urban agriculture in major cities. People were encouraged to grow food on vacant lots, rooftops, and patios. Innovative strategies were used, such as converting old tires into planters and composting plant matter and animal dung.

Mini-farms located in crowded cities are not allowed to use chemical fertilizers or pesticides. The government has established extension offices to teach urban farmers how to create and improve soil and fight pests naturally. People are allowed to keep some of the money they earn from their city farms, which is an added incentive to participate.

GETTING FOOD ON THE TABLE

Since the effects of the U.S. embargo on trade were first felt in Cuba, the government has rationed basic goods. Ration books, called *libretas* (lee-BRAY-tas), were given to each household according to the number of adults and children to be fed. Only goods that had to be imported were rationed, but this included most staple foods, such as bread and beans. It was typical to see long lines of people waiting their turn at government food distribution stores.

Under the Special Period food became the primary national concern as there was simply not enough to feed everyone, nor was there the fuel to transport food around the country. Caloric intake dropped below the required minimum, and some people became ill. To help, the government allowed Cubans U.S. dollars sent by their relatives abroad. It also created agricultural markets to encourage farmers to sell their products. Stores that accepted only U.S. currency and that traded in very expensive imported

food also opened. Along with the urban agriculture experiment, these changes made more food available.

Years of experience with limited or expensive food items has taught Cubans to be inventive in getting what they want. When they need something, they resolve (*resolver*, ray-sohl-VAYR) the problem through barter. For example, a new mother who wants milk for her baby may trade a dress for a laying hen. She will then use the eggs to trade for fresh milk everyday. Today the situation has much improved, and the average caloric intake once again surpasses world minimums.

Cuba has also started buying food from the United States. The U.S. Trade Sanctions Reform and Export Enhancement Act, passed in 2000, permitted U.S. companies to sell food to Cuba, as long as the Cubans paid cash. The first shipment arrived in Cuba in late 2001. Increased tensions under President George W. Bush may stop this lucrative trade, but both U.S. companies and the Cuban government hope it will continue.

A rum bottling factory in Piñar del Rio.

CUBAN DRINKS

The most popular alcoholic drink at social and festive occasions is rum. The drink is distilled on the island and used to be widely available to all Cubans. Today the rum and beer produced on the island is mainly for export or tourist consumption.

The lively *cervecerías* (sayr-vay-sayr-REE-as), the equivalent of a bar or pub once found in almost every town, are now rarely open, and the production of drinks for domestic consumption has been drastically curtailed. The same is true even of the *guaraperas* (gwa-ra-PAYR-ras), bars selling drinks of freshly pressed sugarcane. Ironically, the juice of the one crop that Cuba produced in abundance is no longer available to the Cuban people. There was a time when crowded places, such as train and bus stations, attracted mobile stalls dispensing sugarcane juice and a pineapple-based drink known as *piña fría* (PEEN-ya FREE-a).

Coffee is the most popular hot drink. It is drunk from tiny cups and is often sipped with ice water. Unlike regular North American coffee, it is quite thick and syrupy. Every town has its share of kiosks and stalls serving only coffee, and many customers bring their own cups to be filled, often improvised from cut-down beer cans.

The most popular tea in Cuba is the herbal variety. Many towns have shops specializing in the preparation of herbal drinks. The dark, orange pith of the tamarind pod, for instance, produces a popular beverage after it has been soaked in sugary water for three or four days. The pod of

GOOD AND NOT-SO-GOOD RUM

Rum is derived from sugar and, not surprisingly, has been distilled in Cuba for a long time. During the buccaneering days of the pirates, the galleons that sailed from the Caribbean to Spain were preyed on for their supplies of Cuban rum as well as gold.

The first official distilleries were established in the second half of the 18th century, and Cuban rum soon established itself as superior in quality to many other Caribbean brands. Today the famous Santa Cruz del Norte distillery near Havana, the oldest in the Americas, produces not only prestigious rums but also a number of other exotic drinks. Liqueurs are produced from guavas, oranges, mangoes, pineapples, plums, papayas, and cocoa.

There are more than half a dozen rum factories in Cuba producing different types of rum. The quality brands are mainly destined for export. The bottles that do stay on the island end up in tourist bars and the shops known as hard currency stores where only foreign currencies (except the U.S. dollar) are accepted. The rum consumed by the average Cuban is known as *aguardiente* (a-gwar-dee-AYN-tay), which is said to have a refreshing taste and is neither bitter nor sour.

The quality of rum is partly determined by how long it is aged. Cuba's most popular brand, Havana Club, is available at different prices with the three-year-old being the cheapest. There are also five-year, seven-year, and 15-year Havana Club rums for connoisseurs.

Key (Cayo) Largo and Havana are two Cuban places that spell nostalgia and romance to foreigners. Both the rum label—Havana Club—and the tourist brochure sell this popular image of Cuba.

the tropical African baobab tree is also used in a herbal drink. Herbal drinks can be traced back to Africa, where their medicinal properties were the source of their popularity. The scarcity of imported pharmaceutical products and the expanding local biotechnology industry have prompted a renewal of interest in traditional herbs.

TORTICAS DE MORON (CUBAN COOKIES)

1 cup sugar
1 cup shortening
3 cups all-purpose flour
1¹/₂ teaspoons grated lime rind

In a large bowl, mix the sugar and shortening. Add the flour a bit at a time, and mix well each time. Add the grated lime rind. Blend the mixture thoroughly.

Spread out the mixture on a flat surface with a rolling pin. Cut the dough into small circles with a diameter of 2 inches (5 cm). Shape these circles with your hands so that they resemble patties. Arrange them on a cookie sheet that has been lightly buttered. Bake them for 20 to 25 minutes in an oven that has been preheated to 350°F (177°C).

After the cookies have cooled, store them in an air-tight container. They should keep for about a week.

COSTILLITAS (CUBAN-STYLE PORK RIBS)

6–8 pounds (2.7–3.6 kg) lean pork ribs
8 cloves of garlic
1 cup orange juice
Juice of 1 large lime
$^1/_4$ teaspoon ground oregano
2 teaspoons olive oil
5 teaspoons salt

Cut the ribs into pieces that measure approximately 5 to 7 inches (13 to 18 cm). Wash the ribs thoroughly under running water, then dry them properly using paper towels.

Marinade: Crush the garlic cloves using a mortar and pestle. Transfer the garlic to a bowl. Pour the orange juice, lime juice, oregano, olive oil, and half a teaspoon of salt into the bowl. Set aside about half a cup of this mix to be used as a sauce when serving.

Place the ribs in a large nonmetallic container. Rub the remaining salt thoroughly on all parts of the ribs. Pour the marinade over the ribs. Leave them in the refrigerator for 2 to 3 hours.

Set a grill to low heat, and place the ribs on the grill in a such way that they are not exposed to direct flame. Cook slowly for about 30 to 45 minutes. Turn the ribs a few times while cooking. Once they are cooked, increase the heat to high in order to brown the ribs. Turn as needed to brown both sides well. Serve with the reserved marinade.

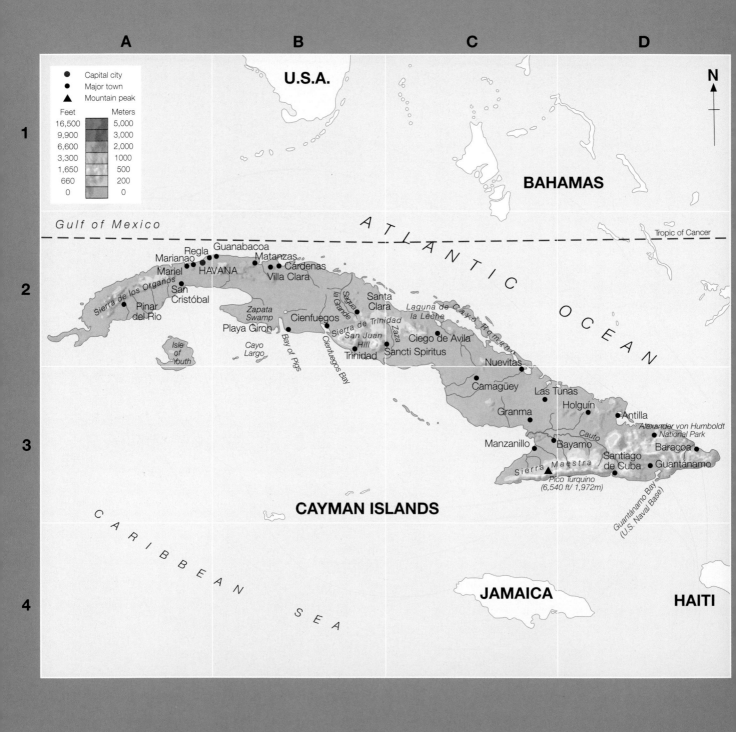

A   **B**   **C**   **D**

N

- ● Capital city
- ● Major town
- ▲ Mountain peak

Feet	Meters
16,500	5,000
9,900	3,000
6,600	2,000
3,300	1000
1,650	500
660	200
0	0

U.S.A.

BAHAMAS

Gulf of Mexico

A T L A N T I C

Tropic of Cancer

1

2

Marianao
Regla
Guanabacoa
Mariel
Matanzas
Cárdenas
HAVANA
Villa Clara
San
Cristóbal
Sierra de los Organos
Pinar
del Rio
*Zapata
Swamp*
Santa
Clara
*Segua
la Grande*
Cienfuegos
Trinidad
Laguna de Cayo Romano
Playa Girón
*Cayo
Largo*
Bay of Pigs
Cienfuegos Bay
*Sierra de
San Juan
Hill*
Trinidad
Zaza
Ciego de Ávila
Sancti Spíritus
*Isle
of
Youth*
Nuevitas

O C E A N

3

Camagüey
Las Tunas
Holguín
Antilla
Granma
*Alexander von Humboldt
National Park*
Manzanillo
Bayamo
Cauto
Baracoa
Sierra Maestra
Santiago
de Cuba
Guantánamo
▲ *Pico Turquino
(6,540 ft/ 1,972m)*
*Guantánamo Bay
(U.S. Naval Base)*

C A R I B B E A N

CAYMAN ISLANDS

4

S E A

JAMAICA

HAITI

MAP OF CUBA

Alexander von Humboldt National Park, D3
Antilla, D3
Atlantic Ocean, B1–B2, C1–C2, D2

Bahamas, C1–C2, D1
Baracoa, D3
Bay of Pigs, B2
Bayamo, C3

Camagüey, C3
Cárdenas, B2
Caribbean Sea, A3–A4, B3, C3
Cauto River, C2, D3
Cayman Islands, B3
Cayo Largo, B2
Cayo Romano, C2
Ciego de Avila, C2
Cienfuegos, B2

Cienfuegos Bay, B2

Granma, C3
Guanabacoa, B2
Guantanamo, D3
Guantanamo Bay, D3–D4
Gulf of Mexico, A2

Haiti, D4
Havana, A2
Holguín, D3

Isle of Youth, A2–A3

Jamaica, C4, D4

Laguna de la Leche, C2
Las Tunas, C3

Manzanillo, C3
Marianao, A2
Mariel, A2
Matanzas, B2

Nuevitas C3

Pico Turquino, C3
Pinar del Rio, A2
Playa Giron, B2

Regla, A2

Sagua la Grande River, B2
San Cristobal, A2
San Juan Hill, B2
Sancti Spiritus, C2
Santa Clara, B2
Santiago de Cuba, D3

Sierra de los Organos, A2
Sierra de Trinidad, B2
Sierra Maestra, C3, D3

Trinidad, B2
Tropic of Cancer, A2, B2, C2, D2

United States of America, B1

Villa Clara, B2

Zapata Swamp, B2
Zaza River, C2

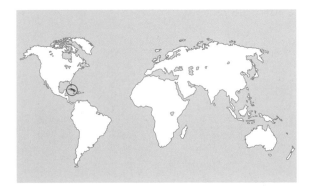

ECONOMIC CUBA

Farming

 Cattle

 Cement

Manufacturing

 Oil Refinery

 Sugar Mill

Services

 Port

 Tourism

Natural Resources

 Coffee

 Fish

 Rice

 Sugar

 Tobacco

ABOUT THE ECONOMY

GDP
$32.1 billion (2003)

GDP COMPOSITION BY SECTOR
Agriculture 5.5 percent, industry 26.9 percent, services 67.6 percent (2003)

GDP REAL GROWTH RATE
2.6 percent (2003)

INFLATION RATE
4.1 percent (2003)

LAND AREA
42,792 square miles (110,860 square km)

LAND USE
Arable land 33 percent, permanent crops 7.6 percent, other 59.4 percent (2001)

NATURAL RESOURCES
Cobalt, nickel, iron ore, chromium, copper, salt, timber, silica, petroleum, arable land

CURRENCY
1 Cuba peso (CUP) = 100 centavos
Notes: 1, 3, 5, 10, 20, 50, 100 pesos
Coins: 1, 5, 20 centavos; 1 and 3 pesos
USD 1 = CUP 24 (April 2005)

INDUSTRIES
Sugar, petroleum, tobacco, construction, steel, nickel, pharmaceuticals, agricultural machinery

AGRICULTURE PRODUCTS
Sugar, tobacco, citrus fruit, coffee, rice, beans, livestock

EXPORTS
$1.5 billion (2003)

MAIN EXPORTS
Sugar, nickel, tobacco, fish, medical products, citrus fruit, coffee

IMPORTS
$4.5 billion (2003)

MAIN IMPORTS
Petroleum, food, machinery and equipment, chemicals

TRADE PARTNERS
Netherlands, Canada, Spain, Venezuela, Russia, Italy, United States, China, Mexico, France

LABOR FORCE
4.58 million (2003)

LABOR FORCE BY OCCUPATION
Agriculture 24 percent, industry 25 percent, services 51 percent (1999)

UNEMPLOYMENT RATE
2.6 percent (2003)

CULTURAL CUBA

Old Havana
Situated on the shores of Havana Bay, Old Havana contains a number of buildings that date back to the period of Spanish colonization. In 1982 UNESCO declared the area a World Heritage Site. Apart from Old Havana, the city of Havana also has a number of art galleries and museums, and it regularly stages theater and music performances.

National Theater Festival
This event in Camagüey showcases Cuban plays and recognizes individuals and organizations that are major contributors to theater. Awards are also given to the best plays, actors and actresses, music, and set. The Theater Festival is held biennially and is an important cultural event in Cuba.

Desembarco del Granma National Park
The Desembarco del Granma National Park in Cabo Cruz is marked as a World Heritage Site for its uplifted marine terraces. Visitors come to the park to view the spectacular limestone marine terraces, which range from 1,181 feet (360 m) above sea level to 591 feet (180 m) below. Cabo Cruz was also the landing site of *Granma*, a yacht that carried Castro and 82 others from Mexico in 1956.

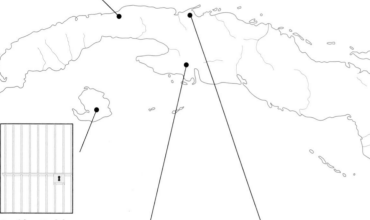

Presideo Modelo
Fidel Castro was one of the many people incarcerated in this prison on the Isle of Youth, Cuba's largest offshore island. The maximum-security prison was opened in 1931 and based on the plans for a similar prison in Joliet, Illinois in the United States.

Ciénaga de Zapata Biosphere Reserve
The Ciénaga de Zapata Biosphere Reserve is sprawled across 1.5 million acres (15,000 ha) and is the largest protected area in Cuba. It contains the Zapata Swamp, which is said to be the only known wild habitat of about 3,000 Cuban crocodiles. These crocodiles are endangered, live in freshwater swamps, and are known for their aggressiveness.

Varadero
The popular resort of Varadero is located near the city of Matanzas. Tourists come here to explore the caves and enjoy the beach and cays. Varadero's waters are suitable for scuba diving, snorkeling, deep-sea fishing, yachting, and other water sports.

Alexander von Humboldt National Park
This national park is a World Heritage Site that straddles the provinces of Guantánamo and Holguín. It is rich with indigenous flora and fauna and is possibly the last home of the critically endangered ivory-billed woodpecker. The park is named after Alexander von Humboldt, a German naturalist who explored South America in the early 19th century.

ABOUT THE CULTURE

COUNTRY NAME
Conventional long form: Republic of Cuba
Conventional short form: Cuba

CAPITAL
Havana

OTHER MAJOR CITIES
Santiago de Cuba, Camagüey, Holguín

GOVERNMENT
Communist republic

NATIONAL FLAG
Five equal horizontal stripes of blue and white, with a red triangle containing a white five-pointed star on the left.

NATIONAL ANTHEM
La Bayamesa (The Bayamo Song)

POPULATION
11,308,764 (2004)

POPULATION GROWTH RATE
0.34 percent (2004)

LITERACY RATE
97 percent (2003)

LIFE EXPECTANCY
Total population: 77.04 years
Men: 74.77 years
Women: 79.44 years (2004)

ETHNIC GROUPS
Mulatto 51 percent, white 37 percent, black 11 percent, Chinese 1 percent

MAJOR RELIGIONS
Santería, Roman Catholicism

OFFICIAL LANGUAGE
Spanish

IMPORTANT ANNIVERSARIES
Liberation Day (January 1), Labor Day (May 1), Remembrance of the National Revolution (July 25–27), Day of Cuban Culture (October 10), *Granma* landing anniversary (December 2), Christmas Day (December 25)

LEADERS IN POLITICS
Fidel Castro Ruz—president since 1976, leader of the Cuban Revolution
Ernesto (Che) Guevara—revolutionary (1928–67)
José Martí—liberator (1853–95)
Carlos Manuel de Céspedes—liberator (1819–74)

LEADERS IN THE ARTS
Alicia Alonso (ballet dancer), Raúl Martínez (artist), Wilfredo Lam (artist), Alejo Carpentier (writer), José Lezama Lima (poet), Nicolás Guillén (poet), Compay Segundo (musician)

TIME LINE

IN CUBA	IN THE WORLD

1000 B.C.
The Ciboney and Guanahatabey migrate from Central America to Cuba.

753 B.C.
Rome is founded.

116–17 B.C.
The Roman Empire reaches its greatest extent, under Emperor Trajan (98–17).

A.D. 600
Height of Mayan civilization

1000
The Chinese perfect gunpowder and begin to use it in warfare.

A.D. 1200
The Taino settle in Cuba.

1492
Christopher Columbus visits Cuba and claims it for Spain.

1530
Beginning of transatlantic slave trade organized by the Portuguese in Africa.

1558–1603
Reign of Elizabeth I of England

1620
Pilgrims sail the *Mayflower* to America.

1762
British occupation of Havana

1763
Treaty of Paris returns Havana to Spain.

1776
U.S. Declaration of Independence

1789–99
The French Revolution

1861
The U.S. Civil War begins.

1869
The Suez Canal is opened.

1878
Ten Years' War ends in a truce with Spain.

1886
Slavery abolished

1895–98
José Martí leads second independence war.

1898
United States defeats Spain and wins control of Cuba.

IN CUBA	IN THE WORLD
1902	
Cuba becomes independent but remains under U.S. protection.	**1914** World War I begins.
	1939 World War II begins
	1945 The United States drops atomic bombs on Hiroshima and Nagasaki.
1953 Fidel Castro attacks Moncada Barracks.	**1949** The North Atlantic Treaty Organization (NATO) is formed.
1956 Castro returns to Cuba on *Granma*.	**1957** The Russians launch Sputnik.
1959 Castro leads a guerrilla army into Havana.	
1960 Cuba nationalizes all U.S. businesses. The United States places Cuba under embargo.	
1961 Bay of Pigs invasion	
1962 Cuban missile crisis	**1966–69** The Chinese Cultural Revolution
1976 Castro elected Cuban president	
	1986 Nuclear power disaster at Chernobyl in Ukraine
1991 Soviet military advisers leave Cuba.	**1991** Break-up of the Soviet Union
1996 Helms-Burton Act tightens U.S. embargo.	**1997** Hong Kong is returned to China.
1998 Pope John Paul II visits Cuba.	
2001 Following Hurricane Michelle, Cuba gets U.S. food exports for the first time in 40 years.	**2001** Terrorists crash planes in New York, Washington, D.C., and Pennsylvania.
	2003 War in Iraq

GLOSSARY

cervecerías (sayr-vay-sayr-REE-as)
The equivalent of a bar or pub in Cuba.

contradanza (kohn-tra-DAN-sa)
A traditional French country dance introduced to Cuba from Haiti.

criollos (kree-OH-yohs)
Cuban-born Spanish, also known as Creoles.

danzón (dan-SOHN)
A dance that is the slower Cuban version of the contradanza and is related to the cha-cha.

El Jefe (el EF-e)
Literally, The Chief. One of the more popular names by which Fidel Castro is known.

El Tiempo Especial (el tee-EM-po es-spes-EE-ahl)
The Special Period, a reference to the Cuban economic crisis that followed the Soviet collapse.

filin (FIL-in)
The blues version of *trova* (see *trova*).

Granma
The yacht that carried Fidel Castro, Che Guevara, and their followers to eastern Cuba in 1956, to overthrow the Batista government. The name Granma was adopted for Castro's organ of propaganda, the Granma newspaper.

guaraperas (gwa-ra-PAYR-ras)
Bars selling drinks of freshly pressed sugarcane.

jai alai
A game played with baskets fastened to the arms for catching and throwing a ball.

machismo
An attitude and a form of behavior that assumes male dominance.

orisha (hor-ISH-ah)
God or goddess in the Santería religion.

peninsulares (pay-nin-SOO-lah-rehs)
Spanish-born people living in Cuba.

Santería
The chief Afro-Cuban religion practiced in Cuba.

socialismo o muerte (soh-see-ial-IS-mo oh moo-AIR-teh)
Literally socialism or death, this is a political motto that urges Cubans to withstand the rigors of economic crisis.

son (son)
Indigenous music of Cuba.

Taíno
Early Indian inhabitants of Cuba, who arrived around A.D. 1200, but declined and became extinct in the 16th century after the arrival of the Spanish.

trova (TRO-ba)
A traditional ballad, once sung by traveling minstrels, such as the medieval troubadours.

FURTHER INFORMATION

BOOKS

Cox, Vicki and Arthur M. Schlesinger Jr. Major World Leaders. *Fidel Castro*. Broomall, PA: Chelsea House Publications, 2003.

Daley, Patrick. World Tour. *Cuba*. Chicago: Heinemann-Raintree, 2002.

Ledbetter, E. Wright, Ambrosio Fornet, and Louis A. Perez Jr. *Cuba: Picturing Change*. Albuquerque, NM: University of New Mexico Press, 2002.

Levi, Vicki Gold and Steven Heller. *Cuba Style: Graphics from the Golden Age of Design*. New York: Princeton Architectural Press, 2002.

Menendez, Ana. *In Cuba I was a German Shepherd*. New York: Grove Press, 2002.

WEBSITES

Cuba: Facts at a glance. www.acdi-cida.gc.ca/CIDAWEB/webcountry.nsf/VLUDocEn/Cuba Factsataglance

Cuba's economy. www.globalsecurity.org/military/world/cuba/economy.htm

Cuban culture. www.cubanculture.com/index.asp

Cuban music timeline. www.antillania.com/Cuba_Music_Timeline.htm

The Ernesto Che Guevara Collection. http://easyweb.easynet.co.uk/~rcgfrfi/ww/guevara/

Fidel Castro history archive. www.marxists.org/history/cuba/archive/castro/

Health care in Cuba. www.cubasolidarity.net/inhealth.html

Lonely Planet. www.lonelyplanet.com/destinations/caribbean/cuba/

VIDEOS/DVDS

Buena Vista Social Club. Santa Monica, California: Artisan Entertainment, 1999.

Cuba Feliz. Port Washington, New York: Koch Lorber, 2004.

Guantanamera. New York: New Yorker Films, 1997.

I am Cuba. Chatsworth, California: Image Entertainment, 1995.

Strawberry and Chocolate. Burbank, California: Buena Vista Home Video, 1995.

MUSIC

A Toda Cuba le Gusta. Nonesuch, 1997.

Buena Vista Social Club. Nonesuch, 1997.

Cuba. Putumayo World Music, 1999.

Cuban Patio/The Music of Cuba. Music Trends, 1999.

Congo to Cuba. Putumayo World Music, 2002.

The Rough Guide to Cuban Son. World Music Network, 2000.

BIBLIOGRAPHY

Haverstock, Nathan A. *Cuba in Pictures*. Minneapolis, MN: Lerner Publications, 1987.

Lindop, Edmund. *Cuba*. New York: Franklin Watts, 1980.

Morris, Emily. *Cuba*. Portsmouth, NH: Heinemann Educational Books, 1990.

Ortiz, Victoria. *The Land and People of Cuba*. New York: HarperCollins, 1973.

Vazquez, Ana Maria and Rosa Casas. Enchantment of the World. *Cuba*. Chicago: Children's Press, 1987.

BBC News Timeline: Cuba. http://news.bbc.co.uk/1/hi/world/americas/country_profiles/1203355.stm

Birding America. www.birdingamerica.com/Ivorybill/ivorybilllinks.htm

CIA World Factbook. www.cia.gov/cia/publications/factbook/geos/cu.html

Cuba Organic Support Group. www.cosg.org.uk/

Ecological Footprint. www.footprintnetwork.org/gfn_sub.php?content=national_footprints

Ivory-billed woodpeckers. http://users.aristotle.net/~swarmack/ivory.html

National Geographic. http://magma.nationalgeographic.com/ngm/0311/feature4/

Oxfam America: www.oxfamamerica.org/newsandpublications/publications/research_reports/art1164.html

Smithsonian Institute. www.smithsonianmag.si.edu/smithsonian/issues03/may03/pdf/smithsonian_may_2003_the_nature_of_cuba.pdf

Taste of Cuba. www.tasteofcuba.com/cubanrecipes.html

The Trumpeter: The Application of Deep Ecology in Cuba. http://trumpeter.athabascau.ca/content/v16.1/martin.html

World Gazetteer. www.world-gazetteer.com/wg.php?x=1105459346&men=gcis&lng=en&gln=xx&dat=32&geo=-57&srt=npan&col=aohdq

INDEX

Africa, 19, 36, 59, 85, 86, 95, 96, 98, 117, 123, 109
Alexander von Humboldt National Park, 57
animals, 10, 51, 55, 67, 68
    alligator, 10
    almiqui, 11
    banana frog, 10, 11
    bird, 11, 53, 57
    butterfly, 11
    crocodile, 10
    fish, 13
    moth, 11
    reef squid, 54
    scorpion, 11
    snail, 11
    snake, 11
arts, 95, 96, 97, 98, 99, 100, 101, 102, 103, 104, 105
    crafts, 95
    dance, 84, 86, 95, 96, 98, 99, 104, 105, 107, 112, 113, 116, 117, 118, 119
    film, 101, 104, 105, 113
    literature, 101, 102, 103
    music, 86, 95, 96, 97, 98, 104, 107, 112, 116, 117, 118, 119
    visual arts, 93, 95, 100, 101, 105

Batista, Fulgencio, 15, 24, 25, 26, 36, 38, 51, 62, 73, 81, 115, 116, 119
Bay of Pigs, 27, 28, 73

Caribbean, 7, 8, 14, 17, 18, 38, 42, 43, 49, 51, 54, 63, 71, 89, 97, 103, 108, 109, 129
Castro, Fidel, 8, 25, 26, 27, 28, 29, 31, 32, 36, 37, 38, 46, 47, 48, 49, 52, 59, 62, 63, 73, 78, 81, 82, 83, 92, 93, 100, 101, 103, 105, 107, 111, 115, 116, 117, 118, 119
Cayo Largo, 8, 129
China, 49, 67
cities, 14, 15, 52, 63, 70, 125

Baracoa, 19
Camaguey, 15
Cienfuegos, 53, 71
Havana, 14, 15, 17, 19, 23, 25, 27, 31, 33, 34, 36, 51, 53, 60, 70, 71, 77, 81, 83, 90, 95, 97, 99, 102, 104, 105, 113, 115, 119, 123, 129
Santiago de Cuba, 7, 15, 25, 115, 116, 119
Trinidad, 71, 82
Varadero, 49, 104
climate, 9, 12
    drought, 9, 44
    hurricanes, 9, 51
        Hurricane Flora, 9
    rainfall, 9
cold war, 27
Columbus, Christopher, 10, 18, 51, 116
Convention of Zanjón, 22
Cuban Communist Party, 31, 32, 33, 82
Cuban Missile Crisis, 28

deforestation, 51

economy, 20, 21, 23, 24, 33, 37, 41, 42, 43, 44, 45, 46, 47, 48, 49, 53, 67, 68, 74, 82, 100, 126
    agriculture, 15, 18, 20, 42, 48, 52, 53, 54, 121, 127
        cassava, 43
        coffee, 43
        corn, 43
        cotton, 18
        livestock, 15, 26, 43, 53, 54
        rice, 43
        sugarcane, 19, 20, 26, 41, 42, 45, 49, 51, 81, 85, 116, 117
        tobacco, 18, 19, 43, 49
    commerce, 25, 89
    fishing, 43, 51
    industry, 45, 49, 129

biotechnology, 45, 79, 109
cement, 45
petroleum, 45
pharmaceuticals, 45, 79
sugar processing, 21, 41, 44, 45, 51, 121
textiles, 72
manufacturing, 14
    cigar, 41, 42, 43, 110, 111, 112
tourism, 8, 13, 25, 48, 49, 89, 128
education, 8, 23, 36, 41, 47, 49, 54, 56, 57, 60, 67, 73, 76, 77, 79, 89, 102, 103, 109, 118
el Tiempo Especial, 48, 53, 121
embargo, 29, 41, 46, 47, 54, 64, 78, 126
encomienda, 19
environmental conservation, 49, 51, 52, 54, 56, 57

festivals, 81, 115, 116, 117, 118, 119, 120, 121
    Carnival, 116, 117, 119
    Christmas, 81, 83, 115, 118, 121
    Day of Cuban Culture, 118
    Easter, 121
    Epiphany, 84
    Feast of Kings, 121
    Labor Day, 118
    Liberation Day, 118
    New Year's Day, 119
    Playa Giron *Quince*, 121
    Remembrance of the National Revolution, 115, 116, 117, 118, 119
flowers, 12
    bougainvillea, 12
    butterfly jasmine, 12
    congea, 12
    frangipani, 12
food, 18, 27, 38, 46, 47, 48, 68, 87, 116, 117, 119, 123, 124, 125, 126, 127, 128, 129, 130, 131